Western Wisdom:

My Poetical Insight Through Poems & Passages

$1R Nuncio

Written, Edited, & Interior Design by: $1R Nuncio

Cover Art by: germancreative (fiverr)

ISBN: 1548285064
ISBN-13: 978-1548285067

Foreword

My loss of freedom over the years has incredibly transformed my way of thinking. I've been inspired & motivated with new focuses & ideals. It also created the opportunity to convey the perspectives shared in this book. Each article in this book is drawn from my personal experiences, those around me, and others I've encountered thus far in life; furthermore, I hope for a better way of life for others like myself. Despite any hardship(s) I've ever experienced, I will always strive for a life lived in peace. No one is entitled to agree with every perspective shared in this book; however, my literature is many individual's truth whether you agree, respect, love, like it or not. There's so much beauty in difference! I aim to provoke thought, incite meaningful conversation, and maybe change the way of thinking amongst the world, but my focus is towards those within inner city communities. I'm pushing for us to live lives for which the dynamics and paths taken to "attain" true wealth no longer highly favor incarceration prior to success. Sometimes.. I believe it's best to acknowledge any great advice given and take heed to the information presented, regardless of the advisor; moreover, I suggest reading this literature with an open mind to be the recipient of what greater good lies within this book. ENJOY!

$1R Nuncio

Table of Contents

$1R Nuncio

$1R Nuncio

$1R Nuncio

1

Life N Tha Trenches

In this corrupt world now majorly influenced by social-media trends, bullets go well with tea, violence compliments egos, and evil passions fuel painful hopes. Finances hardly grow exponentially (legally) due to immeasurable acts of deceit, treachery, and hate which all involve unsavory individuals. Bias views provoke indefensible and monstrous slayings for the sake of curiosity, survival, and greed whereas the compassion for another person's life and/or belongings continues to rise as the most endangered characteristic.

One should not expect to be nourished with healthy inspirations when the surrounding population has been fried in negativity, engages in Bar-B-Que'd illegal activities, and thrives off tangy deeds. One does not often mature tastefully in this burnt environment due to raw ambitions, overcooked aspirations, and subjective dedications. Friendships, which trust builds from lust or the appeal of materialistic gains, marinate in bland pessimism thus never enduring true camaraderie. The sense of loyalty is spoiled and will only flourish with respect

$1R Nuncio

when it is baked in seasoned experience, filled with sautéed values, and topped with sweet discipline; moreover, gallant commitment is seldom rewarded with fresh appreciation and spicy understanding.

Poverty-stricken mentalities desire to be engrossed in wealthy mindsets when they are not entertaining homicidal tendencies. Heavy doses of criminal activity encompass the shortcuts to fulfilling the American dream. It becomes virtually impossible to avoid the overwhelming temptation to participate in the devil's work. Hearts are typically spoiled products unequipped for effective use, and sight is often blurred by artificial successes. A lot of the cumulative beliefs within this native culture are loathed by outsiders and hypocritical to God's law. It is also common amongst the politically-incorrect loose-cannons striving to be wealthy entrepreneurs to live by double standards.

2

Change

Change, one thing which is constant and always in need of adapting to. The outlook of its benefits and/or consequences typically determines whether the evolution in question lies in the best interest of an individual's future or is purely just a sign of the time. It is inevitable, and its final destination rarely reflects its origin because of the detour(s) experienced during the route to success.

Change, one of the coolest yet scariest things life offers. The one who fears it usually fails to prevail whereas the one who embraces it wholeheartedly more often thrives than not. The desire to evolve exhibits itself in a variety of forms such as fantasies becoming fortunes and innovative creations expanding into remarkable empires. Both leave behind legendary legacies. It is amazing how so many people hate to see change make another person's life better and even experience it for themselves, all the while the amount who look forward to taking full advantage of every opportunity coming with the territory continually thrive.

$1R Nuncio

Change, something well worth getting ahead of. Being able to foresee it in its proper perspective can advance net earnings, inspire genius ideas, and make the necessary preparations for a worst-case scenario; however, failing to take heed to its presence and/or relevance can, and will likely ruin an investment at the same time it may cripple a personal or business relationship. Although everyone and everything has an encounter with it, there are many opportunities available to alter and/or dictate its outcome. Being mindful Change is necessary to benefit the most from it and not let it get the best of any endeavor in the process of succeeding.

9/5/2015

3

<u>Character Wealthy</u>

One who is willing to give all and lose everything for a greater good while maintaining loyalty without committing any form of betrayal to oneself, family, friends, business associates, or "the cause" is special. One who appreciates family (rich or poor), values life, and embraces a united team's vision represents realness at the highest degree. One who is spiritually grounded has solidified an essential aspect of becoming the best person one can be. Whether deriving from the heart or the Hennessey, so to speak, it is calculated passion on one's behalf when deciding to act in any manner for which the results are everlasting. It is also quite rare yet dignified when one prefers to speak only after listening attentively; moreover, it is admirable when one considers the possible life-threatening consequences of their advice or services prior to offering either of them. This individual does not take blessings for granted and cherishes the rewards of hard work and unique talent.

One who possesses a grand amount of character wealth stands firm whenever outnumbered by any type of opposing threat, never doubts the power of influence money & sex has on people, and sticks to playing a script many cannot. Trustworthiness, keen understanding, and the passion to accomplish goals with integrity are qualities in this individual's repertoire. This person exemplifies these characteristics plus more daily. To proclaim only facts and believe only what is proven truth (regardless if engaged in war or at peace), requires the strength, discipline, and intelligence only a chosen few people possess. A character wealthy individual has all the above. One who exercises the ability to control one's own emotions while purging negativity is mentally mature. Being character wealthy also calls for one to understand that harsh realities aren't always believable even when true; however, if it is conceivable then execution is possible. This person often produces sufficient results when given minimal information to work with and never allows materialistic possessions to blur his/her vision nor clog the ears, because there is pride in sustaining focus throughout success or failure.

One who is wealthy in character fears no man but God. Character wealthy individuals support and encourage their friends & family judiciously. One who alleviates any issue(s) which may cause the demise of a cherished relationship or profitable business venture exhibits honorable leadership. This person always prioritizes the best interest of everyone and

$1R Nuncio

everything important to oneself, including those respectful of the G-code. This person is fully aware that peace, love, and tranquility are not guaranteed all the time in life to those of the same DNA (based on that fact alone), however bread is often broken without any expectations because giving is God-natured. This individual's morals will not be compromised by acts of sexual promiscuity, yet the heart of this person is open to giving and receiving love from another and never naive of false claims of affection in a relationship. In times of need, other's feelings and thoughts are taken into consideration for being kindhearted is also a part of this person's arsenal as well. This person is unapologetic about his/her approach to life. Being humble & sincere in all situations is this person's nature as the attempt to leave behind a well-respected legacy unfolds.

"So what good is this type of person (in today's society) without the materialistic possessions we claim validates one's success?"

1/29/2015

<u>4</u>
<u>The Value of an Incarcerated Life</u>

"Many of the United States' population is affected by the prison system in one way or another due to mostly everyone knowing someone currently or previously incarcerated. With the high volume of arrests, people may want/need to be enlightened about how to get the most out of a relationship involving an incarcerated individual and avoid certain hardships"

A person's life's value depreciates the very moment freedom is lost to any form of judicial system. For a relationship to coexist and continue to progress (between an individual on the streets and one incarcerated) the person in society must be willing to accept the fact that the bulk of the responsibility is on him/her during that period; however, the challenge of stepping up to the plate doesn't often happen based on the amount of lonely, hungry, and essential-less convicts in need of outside support. Typically, separation doesn't bring forth a quality form of appreciation for the incarcerated because of their physical unavailability making it easier for the free person to neglect the child, spouse, parent, sibling, friend, or lover who is imprisoned.

Unfortunately, the dynamics of communication shift dramatically when one is imprisoned towards placing the free individual's loyalty, will to sacrifice, dedication, love, and respect for the prisoner in the spotlight. Questions are provoked which only can be answered by the person in society. For instance: why do good intentions fall short of execution? Why am I not all the real with myself and straightforward about the "exact" manner for which I'll deal with (whomever) is incarcerated, and stick to it? Why was he/she worthy of my time, love, and blessings when he/she was free but not as a confined convict?

Exercising empathy is a paradigm at times predominantly determining a relationship's longevity in such cases as this one. In the type of predicament being discussed, exercising patience is a must on both sides of the fence. For those individuals accustomed to receiving instant gratification from their relationships, the afforded options of communication (letter-writing, collect calls, email, visitation, etc.) establishes a major problem when and if spending money on such activities is an issue alongside divvying up ample time to participate is an issue for the free person. If the person in society can readily understand how a prisoner needs to be

$1R Nuncio

comforted by his/her love one and truly cares to continue the relationship, it can succeed with effort. For anyone who has been incarcerated previously or is quite familiar with the routine and chooses to abandon someone dear who is incarcerated, there's no valid reason for total abandonment that is justifiable because this individual knows firsthand how she/he would prefer to be treated if the table was turned.

An incarcerated individual tends to over analyze certain aspects of life and is left to assume the worst when communication with the outside world is minimal to nonexistent. When feedback is unavailable, one begins to question his or her own self-worth when considering why everyone has left him/her for dead. Eventually, the person incarcerated attempts to hold oneself accountable for putting everyone in such a sacrificial position although he/she feels no one should be treated less than equal because of their imprisonment.

On one bright side of the spectrum during one of life's darkest experiences, some state one has ample time to master oneself, draft a blueprint for success for their re-entry into society without the many distractions of the free world, and rid of previous bad habits. There is also more than enough time to evaluate prior values and behaviors and replenish the mindset with greater principles to live by and act out.   2/15/15

$1R Nuncio

5

A Selfish Vision

My ego, one's insecurity; my dreams, another's failure;

My fantasy, one's fate; my blessings, another's shortcomings;

Things I care less for one truly adores; my wishes are another's worst fears;

Why is it so I hate what another loves?

At times, I picture crows when one visualizes doves!

One's strenuous endeavor barely reaches the level of success I desire,

Sometimes my natural talent declares me one of the best!

One's rational intelligence grounds one morally,

Holding on to the past prohibits my progress terribly!

$1R Nuncio

One has a humble confidence that makes their aura beautiful, I have opinionated tastes which makes me anti-sociable!

I sympathize with her pain how see understands my struggle!

She magnifies my attributes like I compliment her hustle!

Leaning on me for intimacy restoration,

Relying on her for orgasmic navigation!

Being the steadfast cornerstone of our enterprise,

Her polished mind upholds our status admirably

Knowing her Macnificent better-half epitomizes the grand prize!

4/21/2009

<u>6</u>

<u>The Ultimate Connection</u>

"No title commonly used serves this state justice! It is better than love! It is more spiritual than it is physically yet it's not as emotional as it is mentally stimulating. It is what most people desire and what no amount of money can buy. You won't find it on anyone's physical resume nor can you manipulate it into existence, for it is because of intelligent design only that any two individuals ever get the opportunity to experience it. This something everyone should consider partaking in prior to making a lifelong commitment because without this, it's likely more hardships than mind-blowing heartfelt times will surface in a partnership's path... So, dig this world"

An extraordinary bond is more than just a mutual understanding between two unique individuals in pursuit of accomplishing their life's goals. It is a state of being in which camaraderie between lovers' flourishes due to a strong passion to

$1R Nuncio

please their partner which betters the union's chances of succeeding forever. Endeavors are pursued in unison whether personal or business related. The loyalty is endless and neither person's trustworthiness is ever in question; furthermore, the respect for the other half's opinions, wishes, aspirations, and assets remain a high priority. Assistance is often offered before it is asked for or requested, and the generosity flows exponentially alongside a happy medium of thoughtful compromise.

Great communication reigns supreme so effortlessly that when adversity does present a challenge, multiple plans to conquer the dilemma at hand devises in which the partnership equally benefits or suffers. The union of one another's virtues and values establishes the core foundation required for this bond to endure a life of prosperity. Emotions are fully secured just as financial investments are insured; moreover, a lifelong commitment derived from courageous faith generates supreme discipline keeping the partnership's best interest at the forefront of its connection. On behalf of the selfless compassion motivating each interaction, this ultimate connection moves directly towards the top of a magnificent mountain loaded with accessible luxuries, invaluable resources, and the desires of everyone's heart.

12/8/16

$1R Nuncio

7

A Felon's Vision

It is to my understanding that some financial situations look great on their surface, however true wealth is relished behind the scenes. Integrity is an essential quality of every upstanding individual; therefore, it is a quality surely worth praising because everyone does not possess the discipline, will, and patience it takes to exercise it on a consistent basis. Most morals, values, and principles proven to be incorruptible are universally adopted codes of conduct. Even with the vast differences existing between the many cultural belief systems influencing societal behaviors today, we share many core principles. That moot motto, to each its own, sadly dominates modern day society although it seems to be just a poor justification for inappropriate and/or inexcusable behavior. What one truly stands for displays in action when one believes no one is paying attention; furthermore, verbal expressions speak volumes about an individual's character depth so always listen attentively.

There is no valid reason for one to front on the very people one does not even, respect, and thinks negatively about. Also, there is no reason to lie or fabricate significant details about an experience if being true is a goal. Important decisions should never be made from fear but for the best interest of oneself and his or her family and when the time permits, the world as well. Those individuals whom seek approval from people they do not know, love, or respect are fraudulent.

Being a creator and/or innovator earns far more respect and profits than an imitator and will always be of greater value, so be sure to remain conscious of the fine line separating ambition, convenience, and laziness. Deep insecurities reveal themselves in beauty enhancement surgery scars. One significant contributing factor to achieving any type of success is work ethic. One will only appreciate the accolade if the accomplishment came from serious effort on one's own behalf. When lives intersect business operations one must not allow the conscience to be compromised which is a difficult task and why (keepin' it real) is cherished and respected with the utmost. Ultimately, it takes time, experiences, and vulnerability for one to come to grips with the essence of their own integrity and discover the level of another's.

2/27/15

$1R Nuncio

8

Friendship

(What is friendship? Why have friendships? Is sex a part of friendship? What makes a friendship last? Are there different levels of friendship? etc.)

The term friend is often used too loosely these days, yet it is a vital part of society. Often people claim to not need or want friends, but as soon as they are separated from them friendships are missed. Just because two individuals know of one another from being raised in the same community, attended the same school(s), or work together, etc. does not necessarily solidify their friendship. DNA relations should take precedence in relationships involving non-related individuals, and true friendship isn't a given nor is it granted by law; however, a friend can become family through trial(s). The expectations of friendship need to be thoroughly discussed prior to making that commitment because far too often people define friendship differently. The process of communication prior to any significant commitment establishes the guidelines for loyalty and betrayal therefore clarifying the standard of obligation, responsibility, and boundaries.

Friendship can be two individuals believing in one another despite materialistic gains or possessions. Friendships share a mutual state of mind or faith. Friendship is consistent correspondence and being able to trust personal feelings not to be betrayed. Friends uplift one another's spirit when things are down and out. Sex is appropriate for any two friends who will not break the values of their friendship. An ongoing stamina of trust, respect, honesty, and loyalty will make any friendship last forever.

There is a difference between a friend and a homie. The responsibilities ad expectations differ for the two. A true friend can be like family or treated as such to a certain extent. Friends know your immediate family members personally and are allowed in your personal space- like knowing where you lay your head, etc. A homie is a street-tie affiliation where your foundation is built on the ethics of the underworld and not all the great principles of life. Your outer description does not matter as much as your inner beauty to a friend. A homie cares about what you have and what you can do for them whereas a friend cherishes how you get down and which morals you stand on despite the situation.

$1R Nuncio

The manner how one behaves when challenged with adversity and/or hardship truly exhibits a person's character and gives one the necessary information to precisely gauge their quality of dedication. Life experiences have unique ways of testing a relationship's durability. Questioning the purpose of a potential friendship can assist with its direction while weeding out any possible negative intentions; furthermore, everyone pursuing a friendship should exercise the respect, audacity, and courage it takes to openly express positive/negative feelings and/or thoughts to their friend when longing to endure a prosperous friendship.

Authentic camaraderie does not stem from the cosignatory of bullshit! As long as there is a mutual understanding between friends it is alright for one to not fully accept one particular part of a friend's life/lifestyle just as it is okay for one to disown a friend for engaging in anything one does not approve of, but (only if the right to choose) is afforded by the friend in question. A fruitful friendship does not require that every single piece of a person's life is agreed upon or seen in the exact same light because sometimes opposite characteristic traits click well. There is beauty in difference, and the value of a great friend is based on what one brings to the table on a consistent basis.

Courtship is not friendship! Not yet at least, lol! Being a fellow celebrity acquaintance or receiving a social-media friend request does not constitute true friendship. Neither does a yes-man! True friends do not *only* share the beauties of life with one another; friends are also full-time participants in each other's lives when tragedy occurs.

12/28/14 | 12/19/2000

$1R Nuncio

_9_

Internal Complexity

A gust of mixed emotions swept over a dauntless soul, coercing its careless lifeline and core to evaluate its motives considering why and what is the primary driving force behind its ongoing rage. For hatred, amongst its kind, is permeated throughout existence especially towards the prospects who are inclined to endure prosperity due to the inevitable necessity to balance good and evil. Or to give righteous-living an extra incentive to attain!? Or maybe just to stir the pot!? but nonetheless to motivate, ignite, and incite chaotic reactions; therefore, it is solely, perhaps ultimately for the specimen of life who is being threatened by the evils of the world to meticulously develop an Olympic qualifying third-world strategy that'll produce forthcoming results of substantial wealth which'll take precedence in every process of decision-making, or else the ill-wills of nature magnified by social injustices and inequalities will continue to consummate breathtaking thus birthing the demise of all things possible!
6/23/12

10

R.A.P

(Racism Amorally Perpetuated)

The one born south of the sinner ultimately desires to live well north of wealthy. The battle against the pressures of the world is overwhelming for most individuals especially those attempting to enjoy a life west of healthy. Resting East of peace costs more than most can afford, so journeys take distractive detours inhibiting one's ability to sustain focus, endure gainful income, and continually progress. Some may go left when others make it right; however, it is best at times to get left behind when wrong turns are likely to be taken. People will always be at odds with others when there is not one clear definition for the calls of division in question which is accepted and respected by all parties involved; thus, a standard code of conduct needs to be established and applied to limit the likelihood of disrespectful actions that will be committed without the awareness of such behavior.

The advancement of technology has life being lived three times faster than three decades ago;

furthermore, staying human is become an abnormal, for the new norm is on the verge of androidism. Smh! Lol! The fruit of one's labor is being contributed to the amount of money spent on goods which their value depreciates instantaneously. The evil causing too many problems for too many individuals essentially derives from the differences in genetic makeup. It is cool and common now to sex where one hustles and defecate where one eats; moreover, all the things society once frowned upon are accepted as long as violence is nonexistent- that is according to the media and its supporting cast, and the amount of suckas vouching for suckas. #ThatPart!

Those who are in positions of power (specifically those who are supposed to protect and serve the public) operate unethically *yet* lawfully. Explicit acts of racism expressed by law-enforcement personnel have been on display for the world to watch and analyze, yet no significant changes or consequences have been enforced due to the *wiggle room* within our Constitution. Positive interactions between certain ethnicity groups and law officials probably "*Will*" never happen consistently until the American nation's literature is changed to favor all folks. Lucrative opportunities are not presented or granted to many as they are to others because of the inherent racist-perspective owned and shared by the most influential institutions responsible for the economic status in America. 11/04/2016

$1R Nuncio

11

Wired

I truly believe human beings, the sexual beings we are especially men, are wired to desire more than one woman at a time whether involved in a committed relationship or not. The question needing an answer should not be whether men are wired to cheat or not (physically, emotionally, or mentally) in their marriage or committed relationship, but rather why most people are not being totally open, honest, and upfront with their partners about their true social and sexual desires? The desire to be with more than one person at a time burns in each one of us (in or for one way or another); on the other hand, acting on lust-filled thoughts and/or feelings for anyone outside of the established agreement in place with another is something which can be controlled. Far too many individuals settle for less than they actually want and need from their relationship(s), so they find themselves searching and exploring in others for what they have yet to discover in their partner, or do not have the courage to ask; however, I do not believe we are wired to cheat because cheating is one making a conscious decision to break

33

a commitment made on their own will. See the difference?

Who really wants to eat the exact same flavored meal, finds joy in doing and wearing the exact same things, and engage in the same sexual acts with the same person day in and day out for their entire life? No one, lol! At least not too many people when taking into consideration the high and rising rate of divorce and break ups- all due to infidelity, significant amounts of currency spent daily on the various fashion brands, styles, and trends in competition with one another, and consumption of a variety of different meals being eaten daily. Hmm!? The desire to indulge in a variety of things applies to relationships as well. The expectations of a relationship and marriage have not been constructed by the primitive desires of our natural instincts, for they have been dictated by the many doctrines the clear majority of us are incapable of honoring without failure.

There is such a thing as loyalty without monogamy; furthermore, a person can love more than one individual at a time and is able of ensuring that the person of their choosing remains the priority in their life. Often, we have needs incapable of being met by one person. Since no one was made or is perfect, sometimes venturing out to another person to have particular needs met is necessary to feel complete.

$1R Nuncio

Most individuals are too comfortable and content with accepting the bad with the good in relationships when there are opportunities available to enjoy only the good of one. Here is one solution to the problem of staying with someone you do not want to lose who also does not meet all of your requirements, and be with others: Allow an individual to be there for you in the manner which best satisfies you while communicating to that individual THAT someone else will be fulfilling the needs their not meeting; moreover, an opportunity is presented when the dilemma of wanting another person surfaces to either settle, or come to a new and/or better understanding which requires the relationship to be redefined.

A relationship is destined to fail when one-half's needs are not totally fulfilled by the other half. For instance, accepting bad sex along with financial and emotional security, protection, trust, and great communication, etc. or having the best sexual chemistry ever without all the other integral parts are compromises people commonly make which inevitably causes the demise of the relationship. At some point in time the lack of satisfaction from whichever facet of the relationship one partner deems is significant enough to not live without will cause one to look elsewhere for what is not being given at home. Another key to enduring longevity and happiness with one individual while participating

$1R Nuncio

in an open relationship is coming to an agreement that under no circumstance will anyone else ever come before him/her because there will only be one number one.

"With the truth on Front Street, there is no room for deceit"

2/14/16

12

<u>*Better Than Me?*</u>

"Do you think you're better than me?" someone asked.

An individual may not actually think that he or she better than another person, however when one holds oneself to different and/or higher standards than another person the virtues of life valued differently between the two will eventually ca use conflict in their association; furthermore, particular insecurities of the challenged individual will begin to influence their perspective when an act occurs not to their liking. A person should focus on adjusting, fixing, and or acknowledging the fault or mistake in question which may be true. If not, their opinion(s) of another person will be spoken out of hostility when the situation/issue is addressed.

When individuals' outlets differ, and are brought to the table, an assessment of one's own behavior should take place for the best understanding. Empathizing with the other individual before allowing oneself to feel offended by or resentment towards the other individual is a great way to communicate. Resolve can be found with mutual compromise, yet it typically does not happen unless the desire to be respected by the other person is present on both sides, a levelheaded conversation between both individuals takes place, and/or the assistance of a mediator (well respected by both individuals) intervenes. Unfortunately, there will always be tension in the air and some sort of animosity brewing between the two individuals at odds with one another until they begin to see things in a similar light.

2/16/16

$1R Nuncio

13

<u>Ravishing Ratchetness</u>

How does it feel to be a real street nigga!? The high percentage of incarcerated men and women serving various types of prison sentences across the US nation can attest to most of its shortcomings alongside the annoyance for "the acceptance of weirdos". As Godly beliefs continue to contradict the codes in the streets, media-influenced mindsets masquerade marvelousness and the cumulative principles active within the criminal culture constantly culminate in the destruction of life, liberty, and lavish-lifestyle living far more than they allow participants to flourish. When closely observing the global acceptance of *snitchin'* and *same-sex relationships*, a case can be made that the present-day popular trend has ignited the abomination of mankind; however, the success of advancement of technology and scientific inventions permits procreation to exist without the natural process.

According to many financially free, extremely wealthy, and successful entrepreneurs, the inherent advice about success given to children by parents who are not wealthy set children on the inevitable path of strife which likely will result in old age poverty. Huh! How? Why? For real? Those who only pursue job security often live the life of a have-not. Research and discover how true it is since numbers do not lie. Take what you want from this, but this is purely an abstract twist on relevant/existing events and issues impacting modern-day society which looks to be a spiraling out of control in the 21st-century. *America was built on capitalism.* **We have to be our own bosses!** #Bottomline!

7/19/2015

14

Proceeding with Caution

One wrong dose or consumption of anything unfavorable to accomplishing your ultimate goal(s) in life can damage you permanently, so stay conscious of the fact that everything feeling good to you may not be good for you. There will always be haters and inspirational figures in your life's path when you are doing something great, *but* you will have the final say of which type of individuals you permit to occupy your personal space. Life will consistently present you with opportunities to practice whatever it is you preach; therefore, you are in total control of upholding the reputation of your liking.

There can be an abundant amount of pleasure received from making emotional-based decisions just as you can find yourself swimming in the deepest of troubled waters when not utilizing logic. Feelings do matter! However, your instincts of the future can be tailored to your liking by training your thoughts today. When asking hypothetical questions that require realistic answers to relevant issues it is best to be mentally prepared to respond accordingly to specific situations because of the information relayed and consumed. Also, you can manifest your best personality traits and characteristics to be on display at all times when meticulously planning ahead.

Association brings about affiliation due to the majority of individuals having strong desires to socialize with others whom share similar beliefs, enjoy common pastimes, and are in pursuit of attaining equivalent goals; however, you should not presume to judge another in totality based solely on what the naked eye can see or the company kept. A wrongful conviction can cost you your life, force you to forfeit a beneficial venture, and/or cause you to overlook meeting the love of your life.

Never succumb to the behaviors of your surroundings out of convenience *particularly* those acts which are detrimental to your livelihood; on the other hand, it is alright to be influenced by any attitude or behavior that has been proven to endure prosperity and does not violate your morals. Everyone has to be selfish to a certain extent in order to achieve a professional level of success that entails great financial wealth. Possessing the will to resist negative temptation is a unique quality which affords you the best chance to accomplish your goal(s). When empowered by self-motivation, the joy received from achievement is indescribable.

Character is contagious, so please be aware of the mentalities embodied within your inner circle because attitudes spread like wildfires and you never want or need to be contaminated by beliefs, morals, and/or values which you do not share or approve of indefinitely. You cannot play your position to the tee if you do not know exactly what your position is; furthermore, position can be in the eye of the beholder but will only thrive when it is respected, feared, and/or accepted by its peers and competitors. The manner for which you have earned, inherited, or acquired your status in life will usually determine how you progress and set about sustaining that status.

Regardless of the context of the question asked, every answer is an answer. Even silence is an answer! A seed is planted the moment any subject is introduced, and body language (nonverbal communication) is like 70 percent of communication. There is also a very thin line between sparking interest and implying agendas, so listen attentively and speak wisely. How you say what you say and when and where is extremely significant when aiming to project any motive, draw useful responses, defeat opponents, and/or obtain support for your cause(s).

Sometime in 2013

15

Networking

Make networking a significant part of your daily routine. *No connection of individuals should be taken for granted.* See every interaction as an opportunity to promote your brand/idea and/or acquire vital information which may be essential to furthering your success. Networking should become your mindset, for its entwined directly/indirectly in every facet of human relations whether you want it to be or not. Why not capitalize on every interaction with another person/entity? Consider how you can expand your clientele while maximizing the profits. What you can learn, who you can help, and where you can discover a valuable resource should be the focus when communicating with any new acquaintance. Also, reassess each of your existing relationships to create new opportunities and alleviate future hardships because timing is always of the essence. The key is not in handling the product, but getting a bigger entity to move it for you.

Strive to make networking a natural process by being conscientious of every possible outcome resulting from your dealings with others. Think of

$1R Nuncio

each person you encounter as a potential friend, client, sponsor, prospect, contacts, resources, or stepping-stone that will assist with accomplishing your ultimate goals. **Two of the most valuable and hottest commodities in life are time and information** therefore you should never waste either; furthermore, have a plan prepped to put into action for every future encounter and always follow up immediately after contact since persistence is one key element to opening doors to uncharted territories.

Everyone knows another person and probably more than enough to help reach most destinations. Majority of time it is not who you know but what you know about who you know, and that gives one leverage over another making that individual valuable to your pursuit of happiness. Always retain as much knowledge as possible during every conversation, observation, and situation. Stay active in your answer actions and when you land on a helping hand or piece of advice, try to give without expectations.

Your perception is your reality, and you control the view of every experience involving yourself. You can either see each single union as beneficial or detrimental to your life depending on what exactly it is you are seeking at the given time. You also determine whether one adds to or subtracts from your life, so be assertive for no connection manifests itself. Network!

12/8/15

_16_

Uniqueness

Each time my sight is blessed with the presence of your exquisite beauty and delicious scent I have an opportunity to get lost in those candid eyes of yours which are the open windows to your keen wittiness. Your beautiful eyes exhibit the incredible strength of your character while displaying the pure passion of your soul. I lustfully imagine the sweet taste of your soft lips and gracefully admire the delicacy of your brilliantly-sculpted cheekbones. I enjoy your every feature whenever you're in my atmosphere. The rarity of your feminine attributes compliment your honorable morale, as it is topped with dazzling charisma thus enlightening me to the elegance of your woman's worth. I'm encouraged to value, appreciate, and cherish the essence of your amazing self because you're everything I love, want, and need in a partner.

We must be grateful for the mysterious manner God intelligently designed our lives to emerge. Let's honor the fact that we met at a time when ready, able, and willing to embrace a loving friendship by sincerely and open-heartedly acting in manner of maturity within our relationship. Our interest in one another alongside similar pastimes make for great chemistry, but it is our trustworthy intuitions that give us comfort in exploring an everlasting relationship. Our eager efforts to satisfy one another will shine in moments of destiny.

2/16/16

$1R Nuncio

17

2 Good 2 Be True

With a million & 1 valid excuses to leave,

She somehow found some good enough reasons to stay.

Filled with a high enough volume of doubt to tip any scale,

She allowed her heart to believe the unbelievable was not a fairy tale!

On her own will an unforced self- motivated sacrifice was made

Placing her current pleasures, needs, & future plans on hold for a decade

For an extremely special partner

Who she finds through years of experience unworthy of trade!

$1R Nuncio

Smiling through the stress while laughing off the headaches,

The cause forcing the love to flow fluently through her veins

Is now considered priority and definitely worth any wait!

Never missing an opportunity to prove her loyalty,

She doesn't accept any treatment less of royalty.

She thrives off hope & faith

Trusting she'll get hers in the time of destiny!

Loving like love has never loved before,

She makes it virtually impossible

To Risk seeing if another is worthy enough to explore!

3/15/08

$1R Nuncio

_18_

History in The Making

WE FINALLY DID IT, got that position of power

What we gone do with it, hope the representative isn't a coward!

Reality is, America's still truly scared of us

Inferior, NOW THAT WE'RE UNITED SUPERIOR!

In history statistically, we're destined to have come this far

Vividly remember how hard we struggled for so long.

MORE DRAMA SINCE REACHING NEW HEIGHTS with Obama

But KARMA IS ALL IN OUR FAVOR, and that's on my momma!

I'm blessed to have witnessed the once impossible make it,

Yes, stress comes with blood, sweat, tears, hard work & dedication

The sacrifice of lives like Malcom X & Martin King

Has finally paid off now that *WE LIVE SOME OF THE DREAM!*

It seems, the gospel being preached has a lot truth,

That **BLACK IS BEAUTIFUL** and Barack is living proof!

No matter what one's race is, WITH RESPECT WE SHOULD TREAT ONE

1st Black American leader came from jungle fever (hmm!)

At an all-time high for Black men incarceration

So, **WAS JUSTICE SERVED 2009 INAUGURATION?**

I'm glad to be a part of the living population, Although sad to see **my brother Shaeondogo** McGee didn't make it!

Tears shed from SO MANY BEAUTIFUL FACES

Change has come, love outweighed the hatred!

HOPE & FAITH PREVAILED with precedence

The 44th president of the United States proves *it's the evident*

$1R Nuncio

We have overcome one of the divided states of America's biggest challenge

And **Best believe we're not done**

It's just the beginning of WHAT GOD HAS PLANNED FOR US!

1/20/2009

$1R Nuncio

19

My Stompin'grounds

Very seldom does a dreadful storm shoot the
through the palm trees

Because the blazing sun loves to kiss its residents
and visitors flesh regularly

For it's consistently endorsed by the delightful
shades of a summery blue sky,

Yet smog blankets the lungs of every breathing soul
present; moreover,

The scent of gunpowder forever meshes with the
aroma bomb marijuana

Which often clashes with overpriced designer
fragrances

Diverse cultures and rival ethnicities seek the warm
embrace and demise of each other

As scantily clad gorgeous folks from all walks of life
paint the sands & walkways

Of the critically acclaimed sexiest beaches in the
world which are

Minutes away from any section of the city, in
addition to the

Blue & Red flashing lights decorating sites for hours
of every day and night to

Outshine the high-end fashioned lost angels and the

Assorted-colored and styled footwear parading the
cracked concrete streets

Where few roses stem from and far 2 much innocent
blood dries

Not distant from the redbottoms clicking in stride
drawing the attention of

Assertive eyes competing with blaring melodies of
different genres of music.

There's no greater setting to enjoy a marvelous
sunset that vanishes beyond an ocean's end

And see tourists flock seasonally to indulge in every gossip rags' hyped up activities

While savoring the flavored whiff of satisfying homemade recipes radiating from local restaurants,

However, hollow-point shell-cases carpet the gutters of plenty backstreets

Where every sport team's logo represents a branch of the gang population

Whose locs mask killer-instinctive eyes of the affiliates plus

Classic-American engines roar beside European coupes in front of Softtails

Swervin' behind candy-painted sedans and SUV's as designer frames stare in awe.

When desperation isn't stroking egos in the a.m.

And exaggeration is annoying the afternoon

Jealousy & envy doesn't set the evening tone

Nor does deceit get honored during the night

$1R Nuncio

Therefore, betrayal cannot win the day;

Thus, ambition will fuel days so motivation can thrive for months

And determination will fuel days so motivation can thrive for months

And discipline will reign throughout the years

For dedication to dominate decades

Yet respect will always rule centuries where strength of character is built

To triumph adversities and wisdom is sought and retained to defeat the odds

So the unsuccessful endeavors to prosper illegally will not have the final say

Although the love for this extraordinary place

Often decides one's fate!

Summer 2012

20

My Brother

So many dreams left unfilled and too many goals unaccomplished

So much game never getting the chance to be played,

"Why'd he have to leave so soon?"

How can one be appointed to report to the throne

When on the verge of branching off to better things?

Most definitely deserved more time in life's movie

Cuz' he always stuck to the script of an A-lister,

Played by the rules of the game and never got caught cheating.

Who could have pictured this at a time like this

$1R Nuncio

When he was in such high spirits;

Fresh out of the gutter beginning to walk streets in full stride

And I'm on the other side of the barb wire fence

Useless for the time being with only an ear to listen and eye to witness.

Been through so much with so little experience,

Did the shit he begged to differ with cease his existence?

Based on his solitary profile, some secrets will never unfold

At least he did breed a fine seed

And hopefully live on through Shae'on's soul!

I'll probably never know why until I die

But I guarantee in all my days to come,

Until we can again see eye to eye.

When a SHOTGUN bursts they say it can't be traced,

And anywhere in **Gardena** you smelled the finest pines

Nine times out of ten Magoo was in the place!

I know for a fact he was sick & tired of being sick & tired

But wasn't ready to go just yet,

Cuz' he never gave up striving for some mo' of it!

On that note, *I LOVE YOU BRO & MISS YOU*

And will continue to do it like you'd want me to!

G.I.P Magoo 1/29/2006

$1R Nuncio

21

Matter of Perception

(Life vs Death)

Sickened by a life-threatening disease,

Which has to be accounted for every minute of the day,

But at least I'm not dead!

Not an ounce of energy left to spend regarding facets of a physical life,

For one is only a spiritual being forever in a place unknown to man.

Rottin' in solitary confinement with years left on a lengthy sentence,

Skin dry as *East African desert heat* in July without a soul to call collect,

$1R Nuncio

No music, television, or trustworthy person to speak frankly with,

No opportunity to feel the sun shine,

Nor will the rain ever touch the flesh,

Yet I'm still alive!

No bills to pay, cops to avoid, or diseases to catch,

No friends to neglect or relatives to upset,

No rules to abide by or tears to cry,

Just confinement in a never-ending state unfamiliar to any living being.

No one to sex, give love to or receive affection from,

No one to laugh, drink, smoke, eat, get money, or share pastimes with,

Nor able to bear witness to an ocean's, forest, or city's landscape,

No opportunity to feel the warm embrace of a woman's touch,

$1R Nuncio

For the both are purely out of sight, mind, and reach;

Therefore, one's own perspective determines

Which state of being is better off.
August 2014

22

Lady Macnificent

My heart yearns strictly for the fruits of your love

For your soul is exhibited through exquisite attributes,

Therefore, I desire only to dwell in the depths of your passion.

The sincerity of your generosity keeps my attitude in check

As the tenderness of your gracious spirit radiates from deep within

My utmost sensitive emotions and vigorous hormones ignite,

Bringing about a union dedicated to pleasing you thoroughly.

$1R Nuncio

An undeniable chemistry establishes the moment we entwine;

Conjured of familiar hopes, similar qualities, and respectful wishes we are,

Our intimate needs meet where long-awaited dream-partners unite

While our faith to flourish as one gains maximum strength

The best feeling known to mankind bounds our lifelong partnership

Undoubtedly worthy of your position of ultimate trust

Due to every unforgettable deed executed for the sake of my sanity being accomplished with an unconditional display of loyalty,

I grant you the Queenship to any Kingdom I shall rule.

Accredited with the will to satisfy my insatiable demands,

You're prepared to triumph any adversity hindering our progress.

$1R Nuncio

Horny as the bitch in heat you are,

You're a gorgeous specimen of life.

Born with the competence to shine brighter than most

Considering each of my perceptions regarding you are true,

Every moment spent in your presence deserves a toast!

$1R Nuncio

23

Primarily

When I'm looking for a reason to smile

Your number will be the first & only I desire to dial!

When I need motivation to continue to thrive,

I want to revert to the memorable moment when you decided to be mine!

To support me unconditionally & be inspired by the sincere encouragement

Your honest eyes radiate joy within when we vibe,

Because *any* woman dedicated to "Tha Macnificent 1"

Deserves, and will receive nothing less than excellence!

Due to the importance of every private performance,

I promise to do my best to be the best (you'll ever have)

Knowing the relevance of what's prevalent;

Furthermore, when our feelings become mutual

All facets of our relationship will be beautiful,

From the money-makin' to the backboard breakin'!

Once our harmonious souls entwine

We'll be destined to endure a lifestyle so divine

Disregard every hater who may try to undermine

Your faith in pursuing happiness with a man on the inside

And allow your initial intuition to define

The foundation for which your caring heart will lie!

3/19/12

24

Lady Bird

Naturally blessed with the gift to rise above many,

Lady Bird happens to be supplemented with

A free spirit and unanimous style loved by plenty!

Falling heir to such a remarkably beautiful structure,

Most can't help but admire her features!

Thankfully she's a constant reminder that my future

Befriends an awesome and optimistic teacher!

One curious creature never afraid to broaden her horizon,

She's quietly experimental and accepts difficult challenges

$1R Nuncio

For she's built with the ability to retreat at any given time!

In more words than one,

Lady Bird essentially has an enchanted glow,

Stronger than believable emotionally, so passionate about hers,

Sensual when needed to be, interested in the uncommon,

Only impressed by genuine gestures as she loves life

And all I ever wanted as a Birdman!

6/2/2010

$1R Nuncio

25

Upscale Erotica

Trapped in a silk tunnel of lust,

The epitome of ecstasy is on the horizon.

As sweet sensations permeate love muscles,

Happiness in the form of a sticky substance is encouraged to bust

Due to the welcoming of deep, hot-blooded desirable thrusts!

Tensions releases from the body when the companionship of passions prevail

Velvet barriers of dauntless curiosities seeking ultimate satisfaction,

Furthermore, the primitive act of procreation incites an extravagant tale

As compassionate souls radiate a distinct yet erotic smell!

Soaring amongst satin skies clouded by marvelous pleasures,

The company of tender flesh illuminates

An honorable path to one of man's most sought treasures!

A tranquilizing effect of a full erection vacationing in the softest place on earth

Stunningly compensates a woman's yearning for true love.

When unforgettable orgasms stimulate from a man's exceptional work,

No room is left to doubt the sensuality of a woman's worth!

Bedroom excursions consist of some explicit & unimaginable acts of sexual desire,

For warm tongues bathe lovely figures entirely with special attention paid to the utmost sensitive body

$1R Nuncio

parts along with an array of lust-filled emotions provoking unfathomable positions,

Leaving loving partners spent to relish the burning sensations of hormones on fire!

Bravado is shone through sparkling eyes

Whilst drenched bare chests meet and starving lips taste one another

<u>Consummating life's most celebrated climax</u>!

9/15/14

26

What If?

What if

My flower garden was as beautiful as you;

would it be filled with thousands of 24 carat gold roses?

What if

My jump shot was as loyal to the net as you are to me;

would I ever miss a shot?

What if

I could hold a note as great as you hold me;

would I caress the ears of the entire world as you do my whole body?

If I love my child as you love yours,

I'll for sure be the greatest parent I could ever be!

$1R Nuncio

If I could cook as great as you look,

I'd be the top chef in the world!

If my face was more handsome than your feet are pretty,

I'd be the face of the best-selling clothing brand!

If everyone got along as well as we do,

The world would be a much better place!

27

The Woman So Wonderful

Beautiful dreams of you always inspire better days ahead,

Therefore, entertaining the slightest thought of you intimately

Arouses temptation to enter the bed!

Hearing the sexiness in your tone of voice triggers my hormones vigorously,

And any time taken to reflect on your love

Brings about pleasant pictures so vividly!

One sensual touch during a moment of lust,

Feels like ice sliding down my back in the middle of August!

Filled with sincerity like the passion of Christ,

Ears stay open listening to your brilliant advice!

Hands down with no questions asked,

You possess an impeccable amount of ass, jazz, and class

Leaving no hope for another in the future

Putting shame to everyone from the past!

5/19/2008

28

<u>*Lost & Unfound*</u>

The initially viewed difference between us and them

Should be of the least importance when it comes to success,

A great factor when distinguishing who is most likely to,

Though seeing is believing, be careful of what you're conceiving!

In more categories than none,

Our ups are their downs as their lows are our highs

Although we walk in comparison to none,

The verdict comes from the votes seen only through their eyes!

Deep down inside we may share similar beliefs

$1R Nuncio

Yet what's valid on its face is the hate towards each other we embrace,

Knowing this injustice, we're supposed to act more carefully

Instead we think in manners unconcerned with one's fate!

When will the meaningless cease, some have a genuine interest to know

While the governing founders could care less I suppose,

Will potential allies remain senseless foes? OR

Will well-known rivals war until the world explodes?

Better them than us, resides the motto of the masses;

As abrasive attitudes keep the two clashing,

Excessive impatience forces us to make amends the fastest,

Results must come in action, without tongue lashings.

$1R Nuncio

Unless we're destined to function in this manner!

10/21/2008

$1R Nuncio

29

How to Maintain a Healthy Relationship

Intro to Key Ideas:

It is inevitable not to be a participant in a relationship of some sort. Whether it is a friendship, being a spouse or bonding with your significant other/sexual partner, a family tie, connection with your fellow peers, superstar and his/her fans, one and their higher power etc., we all take part in one of these relationships, right?

Key Idea:

Here are a few methods I suggest for maintaining a healthy positive relationship with your significant other.

Transition:

Before you devote time and energy to preparing, promoting, and pursuing a healthy/positive relationship with your significant other one should have a structured *visible* foundation. (I put emphasis on the word visible just to note that both are consciously aware of the goals and how to achieve them)

1. Integrity, trust, and appreciation are foundations of any meaningful relationship.

2. (A) An outgoing stamina of sacrifice and dedication will note that all can be done within reasonable reality is being done so. **Love does not fail, people do!**

3. (B) Please do not give your significant other a batting average fixed and irrevocable because we are all taking swings at the opportunities of daily living, so if you are giving 132% to the prior commitment you have made all that one can do is accept the deliberate effort.

Transition:

Now that a sincere commitment to pursue a partnership has been made based on life goals and ideals, each partner has duties, pleasures, desires,

$1R Nuncio

and needs to be fulfilled by their other-half/better-half. These must be maintained with direction. Expanding your horizon without breaking your limitations is the goal. The desire to achieve this has to be genuine to endure longevity.

2.   Always look at the facts, make the proper adjustments, and respond accordingly.

(A) Deal with the situation and the situation only! Do not put your feelings and emotions inside the box with the problem and make the matter worst.

(B) Determination is often the first chapter in the book of excellence, and trust is the only quality that matters when it comes down to the wire.

Now to conclude this, I suggest you stay in control of your emotions always even though it is hard for us to do. Stay consciously aware of your relationship's foundation and any prior commitment made. Be sure any meaningless disagreement does not escalate to drastic measures. Do not get caught up with instant gratification and wants, because it is all about exercising discipline to sustain stability.

30

Urban Vantage Point

I smell it, and it ain't so pleasant;

That sour character stench derived from media-influenced intelligence!

Of course I see it, it's available behind every door I'll open;

An opportunity to entertain shame for some change, or do some government whoring!

I want it, even feel at times dues have been overpaid to own it;

I'm after that my kids' kids' kids gone be rich component, and longer than a moment!

Only way to escape the lack of realism rising amongst the living,

Maybe train the emotional state to never be affected by any feeling.

Black-American lives seem to matter like the latest social media trend;

For profit, gossip and entertainment, or until there's a shift in the wind, temporarily!

Systematic oppression and inherent racism

Is real, relevant, and radical as the court of public opinion.

Our U.S. educational system (K-12) needs a change in curriculum;

Courses on financial planning, capitalism, and what to do when shit goes wrong!

The expectations of a felon are similar to the rate of divorce for an American marriage,

So something's gotta give until we find better ways of life to live.

An unfathomable imagination surfaces when one is powerless

And since perception is reality,

What one believes about anything one expresses literally has no merit, cuz an individual is gonna see their way initially regardless!
8/22/15

$1R Nuncio

31

The Pursuit

The excitement from prioritizing a new goal to accomplish propels one's best foot forward in route of victory! The adrenaline rush derived from thoughts of establishing an everlasting relationship fuels the upcoming and ongoing journey! Past mistakes are evaluated as previous prevailing decisions refurbish during the attempt to defuse possible hardships! Resourceful ploys come to mind for the sake of winning at all costs! There is no fear of the unknown, for only an abundance of joy sails an ocean of hope filling the capacity of each calculated step taking place! The receptive aura of the status, prospects, goals, and/or dreams being pursued ignites familiar and desirable attributes known to entice everything required to experience true happiness. The best qualities are exhibited at the forefront of this pursuit, *as emotions wrestle with motives in the backseat of a dream driven by faith.*

32

Below My Poverty Line

Most self-willed and peer-pressured choices to gangbang

prior to knowing how to make, save, invest, and spend real change,

Enables poor financial habits to develop which prohibit productive change!

Traumatization from institutionalization,

Heightens the realization of significant time being wasted!

The thirst for acceptance consistent with that hunger for validation

Mistakenly encourages urban survival based on bad decision-making!

Witty cons calculating substantial math on unlawful paths

performed on oneself first and others last,

And the execution of lawless formulas acquiring cash

prove the streets' math can turn life all bad!

Sex isn't turnt down because of inadequate body parts,

and love still loves when requirements don't meet!

Unwise commitments are often made too soon, as

dedication continues when happiness is felt every blue moon!

Some hustles misrepresent the truth of character traits!

The true passion of intent often gets overshadowed by tone during arguments,

as the inconsideration of others is normal behavioral content!

$1R Nuncio

33

Get It Together

Is it really meant to beef on the streets,

When eventually we'll be ridin' as one in the penitentiary?

They give us power through our music yet only some use it,

While most abuse it and others don't even know what to do with it!

Brewing like a fresh batch, game simmers to make snaps;

When in the end, all that really matters is where your faith is at!

If the focus is on a future that the present doesn't want to have,

Then don't let the past hold you back,

and You'll really be bad!

$1R Nuncio

The matter of fact is - that if we all come together and

make serious endeavors to get the *real cheddar*,

we'd make the world better, cuz nobody does it better

Than the most hated, feared, and loved number one trend setters!

So let's get our priorities together knowing it's very much needed

that we do it for our future generations in respects of those not breathing!

We achieve success with our progress

although the process is stressed, it makes us the best!

3/16/2008

$1R Nuncio

34

Baby Girl

The kind of girl I don't really mind kissing on, licking on,

Accepting hustle-money from or taking home!

She never says no when matters concern her big daddy, and

Regardless of the difficulty, she completes all tasks that'll make me happy!

My baby girl gets everything she wants from me

Cuz she does whatever I want to please!

She's my most requested presence in life-threatening situations,

The lady sought after when my hormones are blazing!

Forever furnished with a distinguished desire to satisfy,

The cause of jealousy in every other woman's mind!

My baby girl, yes! she poses as the ultimate threat

To any other woman's rise in my life!

Understanding as a therapist and witty as a profound artist,

She keeps a distance from being materialistic

Further than the range between the sun & earth,

All the while being extremely sexually gifted.

In essence ultimately, my baby girl possesses

All the needed qualities for a playa in the game!

Appropriately attractive, secretly a sexual beast, and radically respectful

Cleverly compassionate, essentially all I ever need & want

Every time I need and want it!

Ain't a title better to have for the young love of my life

Than being my MF'n Baby Girl!

9/18/2009

$1R Nuncio

35

Fun While It Lasted

One of the nicest yet meanest females one could know!

Housing a party in her pants enticing everyone viewing to dance,

Undeniably she's one helluva show!

She looks just as good as she fucks and cooks even better than she sucks!

With a love unconditional as her loyalty,

Certifying her a true thoroughbred deserving to be laced like a King's threads!

Her babydad's trash and her future man's treasure,

A test you'd want to pass despite the extreme measures!

Accepting the clash for the wonderful pleasures,

She's the sun in the spring after a winter of bad weather!

Decades of contributing to the world her charm

Many fell short tryna grasp her in their palms!

Time must be of the essence,

Because it's the only reason I got her locked in my arms!

$1R Nuncio

36

My 'Lil Mama

So adventurous, wild & sexy always willing to do

whatever

Just my kind of girl

Keeping her heart in all her endeavors!

Struts with an extreme stride of confidence

Like her shit doesn't stink knowing her head-game is sensational,

When she straddles her love interest

Being with her intimacy is irresistible!

Marvelous in the morning, almighty in the afternoon

Elegant in the evening and nourishing at night,

Just like big daddy needs her to be!

Easygoing and forever accessible

Constantly mouthing off something terrible

Equipped with a body so tender, voluptuous, and edible,

She falls nothing short of incredible!

Her youthful immaturity comes with the least expected drama,

But just like some free money I'll never turn down

A chance to have at my 'Lil mama!

9/22/2008

$1R Nuncio

37

Our Flavor

I wanna eat it up, then beat it up, and massage your pretty, soft feet until I'm reheated up

But not before our slippery tongues twist!

My fingertip fingers the clit,

Anticipating thick hips gyrating & grinding on my chocolate stick!

Granting wishes buck-naked in our kitchen,

My lizard tongue commences to licking down your spine until it's missing

Close to where it doesn't belong fishing for the treasure hidden

On the island its visiting that taste oh so delicious!

$1R Nuncio

Returning the favor while savoring the flavor of my sausage.

Allowing it to marinate in your hot oven of a mouth!

Thus, I massage your scalp as your tongue twists & twirls

Intensely tongue-massaging my package with exotic pleasure!

The main event is performed on a California King

Covered with white rose pedals handpicked by the King!

As the California King prepares to please his irreplaceable Queen!

Blissful eyes meet zealous eyes sparking fiery sex!

Then an overabundance of lust fills sacred temples,

Bringing forth all previous promiscuous thoughts & feelings!

Oh! What a recipe we are for ecstasy!

As your back rests on the fresh white rose pedals,

$1R Nuncio

Legs spread eagle displaying a moist peach pie

Enticing my sexual soldier to stand at attention;

To salute the master, do anything to please!

Entering you cautiously all hell breaks loose

And sexual appetites begin being fueled!

Sexual peaks are graciously met in unison

After countless minutes of friction between sexual organs;

And immeasurable touches of hands on bodies stimulate senses

As lengthy, fierce kisses saturate hormones!

8/5/2012

38

A Night to Remember

After engaging in a very intimate conversation at the local bar over a few strong drinks, we decide to act on our current array of lust-filled emotions and shake the spot. Enjoying the cool night breeze in the parking lot along with the presence of each other's company, we engage in a warm embrace thus hugging one another tight while kissing gently. Once we get in the car and drive off, our ambitious hormones cannot control themselves and you tug lightly at my zipper showing interest in some freaky highway four-play.

With the taste of your sexy lips and sweet tongue in my mouth alongside the tender feeling of your hand caressing my inner thigh, I begin to feel my nature rise. Finally unbuckling my belt leaving my zipper down and pants halfway down my legs, I lean back in the cruise control position allowing you enough space to dance at the party you started. Enveloping the head of my fully erect dick with one hand around the shaft and your big warm mouth covering the rest, this oral sex session ensures me the ride home will be extremely pleasant. Stroking with your soft hands while sucking with your hot

$1R Nuncio

mouth and licking with your wet tongue, your head begins to feel like the best I ever had. Before we have the chance to entirely enjoy this extravaganza, I find myself pulling right up on our street.

Anticipating a night of pure ecstasy, we race towards the front door fumbling with keys impatiently trying to get inside to continue exploring our sexual desires. All we want to do is take this sexual escapade to another level, so we completely undress in the middle of the living room.. leaving shirts, shoes, socks, underwear, and jackets on the floor looking forward to the next phase. With enthusiasm, you follow me upstairs to our master bedroom. Yet on the second flight of stairs I pick you up and carry you the rest of the way! Laying on the California King completely nude, looking *faboliscious* of course, I jump on top of you and begin kissin' and caressin' your bangin' body with my anxious hands. Groping one another vigorously, we get aroused even more feeling ready for whichever sexual encounter the night has in store for us. From lips to ears and neck to nipples then down your stomach, kisses rain heavily over bodies causing moans of exhilarating pleasure.

Spreading your legs as far as they could possibly go horizontally, by gripping both ankles and pressing outward, I begin licking slowly and passionately all over your soaking wet pussy. Sliding

$1R Nuncio

my hands up your legs until I have your asscheeks gripped tight in my palms, I continue licking your pussy inside out. Not missing any section of the vagina, I begin to focus only on your clitoris! With your legs wrapped around my neck positioning yourself upright, my hands begin aggressively massaging your breasts. I then start pinching your fully erect nipples as well. As I am being forced to keep sucking on your clit, you begin motioning your hips in circular motions as you enjoy the direct stimulation from my tongue and lips. Your pussy is so wet I can tell you are reaching the point of no return, so I keep busy until you orgasm. It is damn near similar to a waterfall how your vaginal walls release secretions all in and over my mouth!

Right after your foreign orgasm splashes all over my mouth, you pull me up and tell me you want to feel all of me inside of you! I let you flip me over then squat on my lap. You then grab my swipe to position yourself to ride me reverse cowgirl style. With your hands clinching on my thighs you begin moving up and down and back and forth in smooth motions. Next, you slide your hands down to my feet stretching yourself out while opening your vaginal walls for me to go as deep as possible. After enjoying that for a few you turn around and place your soft little hands on my big muscle-bound chest and ride me in circular motions. Our sex is exciting and ravishingly fun; therefore, we begin to get vocal

$1R Nuncio

and simultaneously scream and chant sexy names, "I want yous", and all that comes to mind in such a lustful tone that our satisfaction is undeniable.

Not wanting to orgasm just yet, I pull out and instruct you to stand up alongside our bed so I can bend you over it for some intense doggystyle. Standing on your tippytoes pulling at the covers and looking forward to the plunge coming from behind, you call out, *"give it to me daddy!"* in such an inviting tone. Before I enter you, I spread your big and soft ass cheeks apart. I begin humping steadily with long, hard deep strokes once I enter your promise land.

While slapping your ass, I attempt to paint every wall in your pussy as I pull your hair. I hump faster and faster with every stroke because I love the cushion when I'm pushing up against your ass! I then place the both of my hands around your waist and pull you towards me with every forward stroke of mine. Breathing hard and letting out sexy moans tells me you are very much so enjoying this round of doggystyle, so I pump harder and harder as I aim to give you the ultimate thrill!

Feeling like you are ready to have another orgasm you tell me you'd like to be on top, so again I allow you to straddle me in the reverse cowgirl. Watching your ass wiggle is too much for me when being inside of you so reaching my sexual peak shortly will not be a problem at all. Massaging your pretty little feet as I watch your ass bounce up and down on my dick feels wonderful, and I just relish the sensation as you ride your way to ecstasy. With your hands on my thighs balancing yourself so I can hit your G-Spot, you grind on me harder and harder while letting out screeching sounds of pleasure as you reach your sexual peak. Riding and grinding in more swift motions you reach your boiling point and begin orgasming all over my dick, at the same time I ejaculate all up inside your lovebox. After getting all of yours out of your system, you quickly jump your sexy ass off me and lick up the remaining secretions off my dick showing great appreciation for one hell of a night.

$1R Nuncio

39

Out The Microwave

or The Oven

Most amenities high-priced at face value are not always the richest in quality; furthermore, the prettiest woman may not be the best qualified mate-*that is based on her physical features alone*, and the most expensive car, house, and/or article of clothing is not guaranteed to be the most durable despite its purchase price. Therefore, always research thoroughly before any significant purchase or commitment. i.e. Do your homework on the subject at hand prior to obligating yourself to any ordeal. Balance your options constantly, and continually weigh the profits and risks of every situation encountered to ensure that the utmost beneficial decision is being made for the betterment of your life.

Ride or die only for a cause undoubtedly worthy of sacrifice. Do not put everything on the line just to floss, because at the end of the day we all suffer from the consequences of our actions; on the hand, we do receive accolades and luxurious possessions when standing up for what we truly believe in alongside the harsh consequences. Do what you feel with all you have every time you do it! You will definitely welcome the repercussions of your actions in a more humbler manner when knowing you acted purposefully. Please include integrity and morale in each of your endeavors so that you will stand neck and neck if not higher when facing the best.

Do not waste time chasing tail! Stay focused on getting mail because ass comes free with the cash! Rats stay looking for cheese, therefore if you keep cheese you will always be in demand; moreover, it is totally on you to determine how much time, money, and/or love you are giving one in comparison to what one is giving you in return. Good intentions will go sideways or down the drain when not executed properly, so follow through to the end with every plan and/or goal and be just potential.

Strict discipline must be exercised in order to achieve great success in modern society because there is a lot of nonsense in the world which tempts everyone to fail. *Last but not least*, be sure you always take care of yourself first because only you will face the wrath of the highest power on day! Also, one cannot always do their best for another individual when one is not alright within oneself. No son, daughter, sibling, parent, or spouse nor friend

$1R Nuncio

will stand front and center with you on judgement day; therefore, you must remain consciously aware during every single step taken in pursuit of happiness in the dirty game we know as life. 2007-2017

40

Errythang Suspect!

Since the moment deciding to trust another with privileged information,

Assuming it would be protected sacredly 'til one's final destination!

Discovering one to be incapable of withholding vital information,

Why believe that person wouldn't be just as careless with your information?

From reckless decisions made to unsavory individuals using other people's names in their game

On down to the foolish moves made and lucrative chances yet to take!

The inexcusable excuses for lack of moneymaking, to

Influencing, hesitating, procrastinating, and contemplating.

$1R Nuncio

Whether perceived truly breathtaking or dearly painstaking,

Sincerely pleased when lovemaking or bonafied fakin'!

Janky means to particular ends arouse suspicions

Second guessing intuition, tempting discipline, ultimately begins

The coercing of back peddling due to many unverifiable questions!

Faulty times of arrival plus a thirsty motivation for revival? You Suspect!

Desire for a certain title and elbow reasoning for admiration of a current idol? You Suspect!

Hate towards an unworthy rival changes the perception of a current title!

Awkward lip & fingernail biting whenever nervous?

Sweating heavily from guilt at a religious service questioning the rewards statistics prove you're unworthy of praise?

To envious efforts undoubtedly undeserving of accolades!

Circle of friends to class of Benz!

Addictive habits to permissive actions!

Not a single thing done is perceived without doubt,

To recently acquired possessions obtained for clout!

Good intentions are dismissed without execution

And **some acts of life will never be forgotten or forgiven**!

2/29/16

$1R Nuncio

41

In This Dirrty Game

In this dirty game, bitches are skanless, niggas are shysty, hos are feisty, foes are grimy, and all that glitters for sure ain't gold. Appearance is nothing whereas deception is everything! Know that if you are in it to win it, you may not win; however, always expect the worst yet hope for the best while making decisions like, "fuck the rest" always putting yourself first. Remember that cum is thicker than blood, and loyalty & trust are like endangered species because don't no nigga wanna see the next doing better than him/her. It's a cutthroat society in the trenches.

Even when one is out in the streets getting major love from the freaks to the homies, once them cuffs get slapped on wrists it will be mean-mugs with no love behind them walls which will change one's perspective on life forever, and force you to be tough. All the ridahs and active gangstas end up dead or in jail all the while the percentage of success for hustlers in the game remains equivalent to the chance of a black man becoming the president of the divided states.

Pussy ain't shit but the bait for "lic" and/or another reason for your main partna' to switch, snitch, and/or flip the script just to get you for your grip and turn tricks to pay the pockets of a pimp; unless the pussy is under the instructions of an individual who is articulated, intelligent, humble, patient, and loving. For the fame... a lot of niggas and bitches change for the worst out of thirst for liquid assets. For the right amount change, some people will rob their own mommas main! So ain't no telling what they would do to maintain particular vices. Now that your eyes are a little more open and exposed to a lot of mindsets in the game, it is all on you to persevere with the information consumed true in this dirty game.

42

S.I.R. Guide

(Success In Relations)

In order for one to feel complete, a steadfast partner has to be wanted, not needed, and self-willed to stand alongside their partner until the moment of death despite any adversities. Accepting one's faults, appreciating their talent(s), cherishing their best qualities, and loving their truest desires is essential for a partnership because it shows one values the other. To endure success in a relationship, every positive action should be reciprocated. A significant other who enjoys their partner's favorite pastimes, challenges their other-half intellectually, and brings meaningful difference to the table will always be interesting.

Trust, without reasonable doubt, has to be built within the partnership on both sides to have longevity full of happiness. The physical attraction shared within an everlasting relationship compliments the sexual chemistry. Of course, the relationship's finances must stay afloat, preferably progressive, to avoid stressing over life's necessities. Perception is everything, so the distinction between compromising and sacrificing needs to be assessed by any couple not wanting to feel as if they are settling for less when doing certain things with or for their partner. One can choose to see their duties as investments with guaranteed interest when not thrilled about the deed one partakes in. A relationship striving to endure happiness for as long as possible cannot lose its passion to please nor its devotion. To compromise may mean for one to settle for and/or accept less than truly desired which is unhealthy whereas one can give up something to achieve for the acquisition of another thing of greater value. Anyone committing to another should set aside ample time to communicate their definitions and expectations thoroughly. Life was created to eventually be destroyed, and relationships are no exception; however, the social aspect of life should be easygoing while leaving hard-work for education and business.

2/24/16

43

My Valentine!

Like the purpose of the human spine,

You possess the ability to be

The sole structure that upholds a successful relationship!

I'm the gun, and you're the bullet

Therefore, I cannot perform at full potential without you;

And though you may not have been looking for me,

I'm extremely grateful to have found a love like you!

Knowing love is for the living,

Why not be the oxygen I need to continue breathing!

$1R Nuncio

Me, without you in my life;

Is equivalent to a car speeding through traffic
without brakes on the 405 freeway,

And I definitely don't want to take that ride!

Until the end of time,

I may never be completely satisfied until we share
my bedside,

But for now, let's celebrate this lover's holiday

By being my 1 & only Valentine ♥

2/14/2009

$1R Nuncio

I Will, Only For You!

I'll never get in your way so that I never block your light!

I'll always be behind you when you're pursuing any endeavor so that I'll be there to catch you if you ever happen to fall.

I'll garnish your eloquent attributes with every ounce of appreciation within me.

I'll stand tall by your side as a loving partner during moments of hardship just as I'll walk hand-in-hand with you when celebrating your achievements.

I'll be the trustworthy protector of your most sensitive emotions with everlasting compassion.

I'll ensure that every dollar invested in me returns with enough interest to better our lives.

I'll remain dedicated to assisting the fulfillment of your greatest dream.

$1R Nuncio

I'll be your pornstar anytime your sexual desires require satisfaction.

I'll never ask anything of you unless it benefits the Both of Us.

I'll do my absolute best to hold you down in the manner I want to be held down, consistently unconditional.

Ultimately, I'll always inspire you when your spirit needs uplifting, but I won't hesitate to check you when you're trippin'.

I'll live everyday striving to be your everything.

3/7/16

$1R Nuncio

45

Traits & Characteristics

Honesty is probably the hottest commodity and family is supposed to be inseparable, yet when cum enters the picture the relationship changes dramatically. A lot of people get jealous, however the manner for which jealousy is dealt with sets one above and beyond the rest. Integrity is the cornerstone of any solid foundation and self-motivation is a very reliable asset when one is in pursuit of happiness. Most lazy people lack dedication, and it is not always in one's best interest to be driven by desperation. Why? It is not a healthy combination when mixed with greed and will likely result in the acquisition of a DOC number. The best seasoning for grindin' is hunger! Who are we without loyalty? If you have a little bit of charm in your arsenal, be thankful that you have that gift.

Faith is the belief in things unseen, and the worst poison for an ill-willed individual is greed. Who is to be trusted? How? Why? When? And Where? Confidence is a must-have to put a successful plan into play, and hating on another person should never

$1R Nuncio

be done. The weak-minded right-hand man name is envy, so will we all ever get along? Hopefully! but probably never! So be clever on whom is chosen to be included in any endeavor. Some say the sign of a foolish man is pride, but it is too much in us to always remain hidden. The type of characters functioning today makes incorporating forgiveness into street business the hardest thing to do and why it is pretty much nonexistent. Lastly, the Mary J in the streets does not promote real love, so it is best to keep faith in the highest power.

3/15/16

$1R Nuncio

46

Hopeful in Hell

Imagine not knowing anyone who has one hundred thousand dollars in a savings account and still believing in becoming a millionaire. How about not knowing a single soul who owns the deed to a house and still envisioning living in an oceanfront mansion. Awaking in one of the ugliest places known to mankind still eager to formulate a feasible plan takes the faith and focus of a successful entrepreneur. Searching passionately for a pair of shoes that only stomp in the right direction exhibits the ambition of a Bo$$.

Making difficult choices often in avoidance of living in worse conditions or suffering from harsh consequences displays a level of maturity seen in extremely wealthy individuals. Being loved by family and friends and deemed trustworthy (due to never burning a bridge and being known for following through on all worthy deeds) helps strengthen one's morale during hardship. Everyone has a past and no one is perfect, yet one's present status always brings into question whether everything one has done for survival or success was worth it. Excusing the rest while focusing on mastering thyself is a must when forced to reside on the wrong side of barb wire fences.

Too many people die young living the fast life in hot pursuit of enjoying a wealthy lifestyle. Setting aside ample time to make a realistic and achievable plan for the future shows growth and development where it is needed. Trying to be all about justice and not just ice means one dances alongside the thin line separating what is irrelevant and what is right for the soul. There is never a good day to die hard when striving for the fulfillment of never walking the track on another *big yard*. To outlive one's own parents in the inner city is an accomplishment rather than a given because too many children fall victim to violent acts of wickedness. Too many cold, long nights are spent lonely for not taking heed to the unsolicited advice of an elder crony. Determined to be more in tune with the advice than who is advising proves that a criminal mentality can become wiser.

5/5/16

47

Snitch

A snitch is any person who, willingly or by coercion, assists any form of law enforcement with the arrest, conviction, or incrimination of a crime of another person or entity. The word snitch is a derogatory term meant to offend, belittle, and disrespect whomever it is used against. Snitching does not only consist of assisting law enforcement, it also applies to any form of betrayal against an individual by way of divulging privileged information to another source resulting in a negative effect on the person whose name and/or behavior was disclosed without consent.

Law enforcement gives two fucks about "anything" that happens to the life of an informant (snitch) or their loves ones. Their only concern is solving the case under investigation. Law enforcement will also knowingly send a snitch to climb up out of the hills of Death Valley barefooted just to gather more information against their case/suspect and often when they are fully aware of particular hazards which they will be unable to protect their snitch from.

One great misconception being a snitch is that a snitch gets away scot free when handed a lesser sentence or is freed of a crime. Another is that snitch will only have to help solve only the initial case. Law enforcement will also drag a snitch's name and reputation through the mud until there is no more dirt to pick up. Law enforcement abuses any amount of leverage against their snitch they can muster without consideration to his/her future. When the police or anyone else encourages a person to snitch they are being totally inconsiderate of their livelihood. They're also aware of the dangerous consequences likely to be suffered once the title of "snitch" becomes associated with one's name. Depending on the person or entity one "snitches on" usually factors in on how long the snitch will remain alive or healthy.

Once a person is labeled a snitch that individual is subject to endure many horrific trials in society and/or while incarcerated. When proven guilty of being a snitch by notarized documentation, a snitch is unlikely to exist in general population of the prison system. He/she will likely serve their sentence in solitary confinement (PC-protective custody) or as someone's bitch and/or mission-man.

Snitching entails, a lot more than just escaping one crime and/or prison sentence. To snitch means to destroy the life of another person and the livelihood of the surrounding lives of that individual. Laying up pillow-talking to a significant other is another form of snitching if the information being shared will ultimately cause the demise of another person's freedom.

FYI: Moral of this passage is... don't speak on no one's business or even your own if there's any chance negative results will follow!

48

My Repertoire

I have the strength, ability, and skills to protect and always ensure my significant other feels secure. My logical thought process keeps my relationships grounded in pivotal moments in which unstable emotions tend to influence irrational behaviors. I provide the emotional stability needed for one to trust wholeheartedly. I have the talent, ambition, and intelligence to succeed in any career of my choosing. My fashion sense and physical attributes compliment the beauty of my partner when attending public events, forever making my better-half look better than the average attendee. I make my love feel sexy and desired like I'm supposed to because my passion to please remains eagerly ready to satisfy all intimate needs. I have enough energy to keep the love of my life feeling young, alive, intrigued, and appreciated longer than ever expected. I communicate with a level of understanding that affords my relationships (business & personal) the best chance to triumph any adversity attempting to derail its journey. I am the attentive listener whenever my ride or die needs to be heard. I keep encouraging words in my verbal arsenal ready to console and/or uplift the concerns of my main squeeze because being supportive and compassionate is my specialty. My tongue stays energized enough to escort the sexual spirit to ecstasy at any time or anyplace. I also have a street-savvy history of operating amongst the most savage criminals which has gained me the wisdom and experience to help children and misguided individuals to avoid succumbing to negative temptations.

<u>Am I who you truly desire?</u>

<u>6/13/2016</u>

49

Divided Shades

Within Divided States,

Our United States

The current state of humanity within America (stemming from far too many years of injustice, oppression and disrespect towards African-Americans) is due to the manner the country was founded upon; however, despite "everything" endured negatively by African-Americans, there are plenty enough opportunities available *now* for us to explore whichever realm of life desired. There are numerous means to generate legitimate income due to the countless sacrifices made over time by courageous individuals and groups of people who fought for equality. Before Africans were slaves in America, we were kings & queens and inventors of life's most significant essentials. One would think that the struggle for freedom in America by our ancestors would inspire, motivate, and encourage us

$1R Nuncio

to be more united, yet we kill one another in the U.S. at an alarming rate while making up over one-third of the incarcerated population.

We should never hate on nor prohibit a fellow African-American from getting their fair share of the American Pie especially when everyone else is against our progression. Since the death of the Black Panther Party during the 1960's Civil Rights movement, the birth of Crip & Blood gangs in Southern California and rise of Vicelord & Disciple organizations in the Midwest, we have been at each other's throat like never before. We cause much more pain to ourselves, love ones, and others than it does feel good when we ride down on one another. It makes no sense or cents to continue living in such a destructive manner! We cannot expect others (meaning the government and law officials and other ethnicities) to respect us with the utmost when we disrespect one another right in their faces every chance we get. The manner we kill one another (whether it be over money, drugs, or gang rivalry) is nothing to be proud of. We now have enough influence in regards to how society thinks, talks, dresses, acts, and lives that if we utilize the vessels of music, literature, social-media, and media outlets to our advantage we could become the majority.

We have to start holding ourselves accountable and to a higher standard beginning by valuing our

$1R Nuncio

lives more. We need to begin highlighting and celebrating acts of intelligence instead of glorifying foolish activities. Ducking cops & gunshots and living in cellblocks is not conducive to experiencing true wealth and happiness, so it is imperative that our perspectives about how to achieve success changes dramatically. It is amazing, yet quite astonishing how African-American men are arguably the most desired preference for the modern-day white woman after being the forbidden spice of life for so many years. The progression and success of hip-hop music alongside the popularity of professional athletes has lessened the gap between black and white Americans. The advancement of film technology sheds light on the bias, prejudice, and racist ways our government, law enforcement, and industry executives still treat African-Americans regardless if they are wealthy or poor. For every bridge built and crossed just as many have burned and are still burning; therefore, the fight for equality will and can never cease. Unfortunately, it seems that African-Americans being equal with whites in America may never be because life is not meant to be fair. Lastly, the best thing for any Africa-American to do is find their lane, embrace it wholeheartedly, and execute every task it entails while keeping faith in their hustle and cause(s) because hoping another person of another ethnicity changes the world for us is out!

6/15/16

$1R Nuncio

50

Your Perception, Your Reality

Success without expensive materialistic possessions is like sex without orgasming; Cool, but not satisfying! What type of love exists without trust? Not the real kind! Not having integrity is equivalent to moral bankruptcy, so one should not believe financial security guarantees a relationship's longevity. Confidence without intelligence is a form of beautiful incompetence; furthermore, ensuring what "catches" your attention has enough substance to "keep" your attention before dedicating your life to one is an irresponsible act of immaturity. See what happen once Eve bit that glossy apple!? Lol! Real talk tho! The difference of beauty on screen or in paint versus beauty fresh out the shower is not God's work. It's funny how beauty looks better when it is famous, and amazing how a car drives smoother when you're the owner.

7/29/16

51

My Significant Other

In every shooting star across the sky, in each rain drop falling on the earth's floor, I see your gorgeous face!

Whenever the sun shines on my face or the moon glows and the wind brushes across my flesh, I feel your gracious presence!

Any step I desire to take and decision I make from this day forward will be motivated by my passion to please your every need!

Each breath I breathe and beat of my heart grants me an opportunity to embrace your love, taste your tenderness, and admire your beauty, for you're the most intriguing & interesting person I've come to know.

My dreams are now fascinating because they're encompassed with brilliant ideas on the brink of coming to a life shared with you!

A thought of you is now one of my life's great pleasures!

$1R Nuncio

Success will be inevitable with you as partner!

Failure seems unfathomable with you as a friend!

Ecstasy will be unavoidable with you as a lover!

Wealth in every aspect of life is attainable with you as a wife!

An angel was birthed in the best month of a great year and was destined to find her way into my arms!

What's missing, what haven't I covered? The physical intensity under & on top of the covers which we owe it to our incredible bond to discover!

Whether this poetical notice to you is deemed corny or clever, the reality unveiled affords us a choice to make that'll determine our forever!

August 2016

52

Between Blurred Lines

There is no difference between a man flossin' in an expensive whip which he does not own as if he is wealthy and a woman flaunting her surgically-enhanced body around town like she is truly beautiful. Hindsight proves how super-quick, defensive responses to inquisitive statements and/or questions definitely raise more suspicion about the guilt of the alleged culprit. Once any type of question is asked or an accusation is made every form of response becomes some sort of an answer, so be extremely thoughtful and careful when communicating because nonverbal communication speaks volumes about a person's unspoken thoughts and/or feelings. The clothing designers who claim to desire for *everyone* to wear their brand and feel great when doing so are living contradictions because if they only use individuals who are beautiful by media standards to model their attire and not average, common, fat, so-called ugly, or out-of-shape individuals.

It is so unfair to oneself and others to prematurely judge and convict the purity of an individual's intentions based on the behavioral history of another person. When dealing with matters of protest, far too often the type or style of protest takes precedence over the reason(s) behind the protest. Oppression, racism, and prejudice is undoubtedly in effect when two human being's credentials are equivalent, and their ethnicity is commonly favored and they are not judged equally. Unsolicited advice often has a hidden agenda or ulterior motive, or is an insecure expression in need of acceptance? The future of a friendship or business partnership will forever be in question when one believes in the exploitation of another's business or secret.

Keep ya' head on a swivel driving in your rearview as you keep an eye out for the snakes!

53

Dear Lord,

Who in the most bitter moments of passion, showed an ardent thirst for souls, I'm asking?

Give us the light to grow in knowledge in your word, and grant us the strength to stay polished.

I know that my life is not my own, but by your death and resurrection you've made me your own.

Show me again that there is love, forgiveness, and mercy.

Use me in the spite of my doubt, for you are needed with urgency.

Teach me to trust in the spirit, give me the wisdom to comprehend the word and not just hear it.

Amen!

$1R Nuncio

54

Vision

Key Quote:

"Conceive it in your mind, believe in your heart, and it will show through your actions"

Being able to foresee the outcome of a situation especially a productive one is not a gift that everyone has been blessed with, but it is imperative when blueprinting a script to any foundation longed to be secure and profitable. To formulate a business, navigate a world, prepare to succeed, and accomplish goals and plans, one needs to be able to picture the situations which are going to be faced, confrontations possibly encountered, and struggles likely to be up against. Try keeping a plan A, B, and C to hurdle any challenges and become triumphant at whatever it is trying to be done. Taking control of the ideas imagined and putting them into the perspective of a realistic form can be the beginning of your own enterprise if you apply the right amount of pressure, stay consciously aware, and do not let your innermost thoughts go afloat and unnoticed.

55

In The Closet

Key Quote:

"What goes on in the dark, will come to the light"

It is best that you stay true within, even when you think nobody is paying attention. What you do behind closed doors will surface more than likely when you least expect it, and the consequences and repercussions that come will not be in your favor. It is proven that true colors will be shown so do not even start believing that you will get away with being fake forever. The profits of being fake are devastating to careers and relationships and will never be more pleasing than the rewards received from keeping it real. Always know that a situation always presents itself that will call your bluff and put the real business on front-street. One of the most precious and important things owned by man is his name and with that comes a reputation, so I suggest if you care to keep any respect it is best you act accordingly "24/7 365" even when you are alone.

56

Good Intentions

Key Quote:

"Do not be resistant! Stay persistent, and be willing to do whatever it takes to walk the distance"

When not followed through, good intentions will go bad and can leave whomever a wreck as if you defeated your purpose. Once you have conjured up the idea, set an accomplishable goal/plan to achieve in a realistic time period, put it on paper! Blueprint your script to success so you do not forget and stay ambitious, determined, and focused all the way through! The key is longevity! Do not let all the energy you used to hustle be a waste once you get what you wanted. The key is to be triumphant while maintaining that triumph status. Do not forget that this is life and nothing goes 132% smooth, so be prepared to hurdle any obstacle threw in your path. Adversity is where your determination and endurance kicks in. Success would not be appreciated without struggle; therefore, it is all a test to prove that the strong survives. If it was too easy and accomplishable for everyone there would not be ranks or classes. Someone has to lead and someone has to follow, and situations are brought into our lives to determine who is qualified to be on top.

57

<u>The Sacrifice for Change</u>

Key Quote:

"Don't set me up, back me up"

In order for change to come about there has to be a sacrifice made. In these times, most are not willing to sacrifice the welfare of today for a terrific tomorrow; more than likely, that is partly why (some) things are still the same in your neck of the woods. Although everyone constantly complains about the needed difference in today's society we as a whole are not stepping up to the plate and riding for the cause of improvement all the way down to the wire.

Who would the president be without congress? Who would a general be without his foot soldiers? Someone has to lead and someone has to follow, therefore both are needed to achieve victory. Two are better than one. Typically, unions are sufficiently rewarded for their labor for if one falls the other will lift up his/her companion, but woe to one who is alone when failing for that individual has no one to help him/her up. Again, if two lie down together they will keep warm; however, one *can* be warm alone.

When the stand is taken by any courageous individual with the wisdom and audacity to finally cease what is not right and make a progressive step forward... **Support**! Do not turn your head and walk away because the problem will continue. You will be singing the same sad song when you had the opportunity to alleviate the nonsense. Know that with sacrifice you may put something as valuable as your life in jeopardy, but the triumph of riding for the right cause will be beneficial for a lifetime to those you love, your soulmate, and maybe the future generations to come.

58

"Thinkin' Out Loud"

Don't Fight the Feeling

What is F.T.F (Fight The Feeling)? Why would anyone F.T.F? When does F.T.F begin? How do you F.T.F? What might be missed when F.T.F?

F.T.F is being in denial or contradicting oneself of beliefs within. F.T.F is beating around the bush or procrastinating during the pursuit of happiness. One may F.T.F due to fear of love or be frightened of the feelings that may come about. One may F.T.F because a faulty situation occurred which one has no control over the outcome. One starts to F.T.F when the shit hits the fan right in one's face and the decision will be do or die. One may begin to F.T.F when their significant other is breathing down their neck and the response is crucial. One can F.T.F by rambling words when a conversation is tense. One may also F.T.F by retreating from a particular situation. One may miss out on the luxury of love for a lifetime with a soulmate. One may also miss out on the great satisfaction of content feelings when

choosing to "Fight The Feeling!"
2/10/2001

$1R Nuncio

59

Intimacy

What is intimacy? Why is intimacy needed? When is intimacy appropriate and where? How should intimacy be approached?

Intimacy is the participation of sexual actions, speech, and/or body gestures without actual penetration. One can be intimate in conversation to let their companion know that sex is of current interest. Signs of Intimacy initiate the arousal of one's own hormones enticed by a particular look or touch from a partner. Typically, one waits to be intimate until love has genuinely surfaced or deep feelings for a companion have developed. Other times intimacy comes natural with chemistry. Individuals get intimate when their hormones desire satisfaction or wish to explore their significant other's legacy. Intimacy can be appropriate at any place desirable and comfortable by both partners. Intimacy usually follows a certain sexual vibe or mental connection.   2/18/2001

$1R Nuncio

60

Freedom

What is Freedom? Why should we have Freedom? Is Freedom important?

Freedom can be the ability to be able to act, speak, and think peacefully on your own will. Freedom could be anything you want it to be as long as one is operating in a free state of mind. Freedom is a choice made not based on someone else's opinion. We should have freedom because everyone is entitled to do what they want as long as their actions and/or speech does not offend anyone. Freedom can be very important if one is someone who does not like to be treated less than deserved to be treated. One might not realize how important Freedom is until it is taken. Freedom is important because it gives the opportunity to achieve dreams.

12/21/2000

$1R Nuncio

61

Love vs Lust

What is love/lust? What do we love/lust? Why do we love/lust? How do we love/lust? When do we love/lust?

We might love one's ability to please or lust another's physical attributes? Love may be unconditional feelings for someone. Lust might be the mindset consumed of sexual thoughts of someone. We love an individual's characteristics and qualities! We lust the fulfillment of another's capabilities to perform sexually! One may love another to create a special bond to explore. One may lust the rewards of a particular fantasy to be fulfilled by certain individual. At times, we love through various forms of appreciation. Other times we lust in conversation, by eye contact, or pure thought. When True Love is felt most never wish to part ways with it.

9/26/2000

$1R Nuncio

All That Glitters Ain't Gold

Key Quote

"Appearance is nothing, deception is everything!"

Think back to the times when the serpent persuaded, peer pressured, influenced, conned, (whatever you may call it) Eve to do the one thing she was instructed not to do. The shiniest, glossiest apple in the tree was the bait for corruption. Just because something or someone looks good and might be or taste even better does not guarantee such. Since every decision counts, it will be to your advantage to research thoroughly *everything* you are going to have your hands on. Just because he/she looks good, dresses fly, and drives a fancy car does not solidify one as a star. The car might not be theirs or paid for, their house might be messy and unsanitary, and because one keeps an extraordinary appearance does not mean that individual isn't lazy, untrustworthy, or illiterate. Do not be in a rush to indulge in sex and fall in love. Everyone driving a

148

fancy car with rims is not ballin', and just because one may have a little something to show for today does not mean they have longevity. More than likely majority of the population you witness having a good time is working strenuous hours daily just to maintain that front.

short-term gratification or long-term moneymaking?

Sometimes we have to substitute the things we like for the things we need, and what we need is financial stability, not to be rich for one good week. "Catch my drift?" To sacrifice a couple of years to endure success for the remainder of a lifetime will be difficult, but it is needed when seeking to obtain great wealth and a peace of mind.

63

Motivation

Key Quote:

"If the profits don't override the risk, it's not worth it!"

Stay focused on your paper and continue to keep your distance from the haters. Snitches are like snakes slithering through the grass, and you will not see or feel them until they affect your health and wealth. Be extremely careful around certain people when you step. Always keep in mind that everybody does not need to know everything, and everybody is not built for everything. Make sure you keep a safety net on everything valuable.

Even Jesus (the greatest man to walk earth) utilized twelve disciples to help spread the gospel, so do not think for one second that you have to or can succeed literally alone. It does not mean be dependent on others, but networking with people for/of the same purpose is highly recommended and takes a burden off your shoulders in the long run.

Sometimes you have to put honesty to the side because it will be unsafe when you are the only one valuing loyalty, honesty, and trust while everyone else around is not caring at all. Just because an individual has proved their loyalty does not mean one can be foul and continue to be accepted and respected based solely on the title of the bond initially created. Never allow yourself to be content, unless it is notarized that you and your immediate family members are secure and insured financially when there is an opportunity to get, have, and do some more (which there always is). Stay ambitious while continuing to strive to be your best no matter what situation presents itself, and know that there is always a solution where there is a problem; moreover, there is always an exit to every entry although it may not be as soothing and quick. Have faith and remember that God will never put you in a position that you cannot handle.

~try not to be a killa!~

$1R Nuncio

64

Something 2 Think About

Know that all friends are important,

and every decision counts.

The selection to be nonviolent or nonexistent

is very significant in order for positive change to come about!

If your speech contradicts your way of living,

the voice of your good intentions will be hard to follow.

The fact that we won't prevail without salvation from God, for some is hard to swallow!

If all men are created equal, then why so much favoritism?

$1R Nuncio

It's funny how individuals with the most faith &
positive outlooks receive the most criticism;

In order for unity to coexist publicly,

we have to find peace within personally!

Everything happens for a reason,

but note how some dreams do come true;

It's also very possible to manifest your destiny,

and the starting date to enjoy harmony

as a whole is totally up to you!

MLK Day 2004

65

Open

Why don't I keep in touch more often,

when it feels so good inside when we communicate?

Am I foolish for keeping my physical distance

knowing it's nothing better than to see

our bodies clash in harmony!

Your humor, your style, your smile just happens to drive me wild,

but irks my nerves when realizing together we're not in route.

Can't call it love

because my heart has no say so with this dealing!

It's a blessing that this site has come into view

and to know you were the cause leaves me in awe.

I'm so intrigued when diggin' your company in the midst of your presence like no other before you

It's unexplainable how I'm considering staying away!

8/1/2005

66

My Precious Lady

Considered bland when surveyed by the public opinion,

Flavored like a 5-Star meal to anyone paying special attention!

They thought you'd stay a dead weed in the cracks

Never to be the greenest grass on the street;

Now look how the concrete rose has blossomed,

I see why they don't get paid to think!

With you in sight... It's like paradise to the underworld

I'm not ashamed to admit... You top the Richter Scale when you score!

$1R Nuncio

Far from filthy, so wet & silky

You're like ice water on a sunny day;

I'm nothing without you-

I'm cereal waiting on you to milk me!

One in a million... I guess I hit the jackpot

For everyday you're in my life I'm thankful for what I got!

8/14/2005

67

My Boo

Never could I imagine, we'd be in this position

Sharing a love like no other, with no limits and unconditioned!

The sparkle in your eyes

Arouses the feelings I never knew I had;

And every moment that I think of you

I can't help but smile knowing you're all I have!

Not a day goes by I don't appreciate you being in my life;

If anything I've done has been wrong, the decision to be with you is right!

Never should we part from this special bond created;

$1R Nuncio

It's no doubt in my mind that together we'll always make it!

Never leave my side... and I promise to do the same

The love I have for you... in my heart will always remain!

8/18/05

68

Visionaryish

How am I able to maintain my sense of self,

   Being incarcerated for so many years as a young man?

How am I able to cease my wicked ways,

   And utilize my most exquisite characteristics?

How am I able to follow through with my good intentions,

   In an unsanitary, immature state-of-mind place of living?

How am I able to value and appreciate

   Loyalty... Honesty... Trust?

   When everybody around me don't give a fuck!

How am I able to give the one I choose ultimate pleasure

   With no prior hands-on experience?

$1R Nuncio

How am I able to obtain great wealth,

keep a peace of mind

and formulate plans to stack grands?

How am I able to remain cool, calm, & collective

Around the best fools

And not go belligerent?

How am I able to control my emotions

And not allow my feelings to intervene with business?

How am I able to blueprint my route to success

Being confined to the underworld and

Derived of my freedom?

~ Vision~

9/1/2005

69

A Moment in Mind

Crumbling erbs tryna calm nerves,

I find myself impatiently waiting to

Enjoying moments I deserve;

The visible interactions I'm contemplating

Whose presence is comforting or absurd,

Safety damaging or financially inflating!

Stimulated from natural resources provided

For the sake of our wellbeing

For the purpose of conquering by division,

I have to acknowledge the trouble I'm seeing,

Examine & execute to make known the untitled,

Unless I prefer to allow continuous fleeing!

$1R Nuncio

Confused, rather unmotivated to proceed with

Intentions to make the situation better;

Entertaining that which is not a benefit

Should be followed through only if rewarding, not more pressured;

Frivolous activities have to be excluded in order to endure profits!

So, is this really worth an endeavor?

Consciously aware of the outside influence,

Determined to make a difference for a positive outcome,

Knowing false outlooks need not to be seen as the truest

While in route to be the recipient of unlimited funds.

For there are several ways to bestow the "do-it-fluid"

I will commit to the path of my destiny, Triumphant!

9/25/2005

70

Our Days Before Change

Pleasant memories with you yesterday

Feel like vivid pictures of today,

Being that you're a positive, motivating force in my life as we speak!

Like lasagna without cheese

or church without a preacher in the pulpit,

You without me just ain't right,

and me without you will be for us uncivilized!

Why would you burn down the car

that helped you reach your destination?

or tear up the leather on the couch

that was afforded to you to rest your tired feet?

Spectacular comes to mind when looking in your eyes,

I suppose your father stole stars from the sky when he made them!

My second wind,

The strength in the pride that won't let me die,

Gir!l You blow my mind!

But the minute you begin to slack in your stroke,

Up,up, up and away I go!

~How I want to stay grounded~

10/4/2005

$1R Nuncio

71

Mz. Significance

Along with the wind,

May my love brush across your path

Soothing your soul and bringing warmth to the heart

That has allowed me the opportunity to keep secure!

An essence to my life that I value

To the highest degree I respect

All that is offered for me to take advantage of,

I most definitely won't take for granted nor neglect!

I figure moms was silk in the split due to the texture
of your soft skin!

$1R Nuncio

Sweeter than a tooth in a mouth full of candy,

and you wonder why I keep a craving for you...

Cold as 1000 karats of platinum under a bucket of ice,

and you question why I want you all over me

When the sun is out shining upon us!

Can't take nothing from you

Or place anyone above you,

All I'm suggesting is that you continue to let me love you...

10/7/2005

72

How I Can Make My Future Great

(May 24, 1991 10yrs old)

I can make my future great by completing my whole education. This includes college where I will major in business and foreign languages.

When I'm in college at Harvard I will enjoy taking Spanish, French, and German. By taking these languages I can better myself, and I can communicate with people in other countries. As for my business courses I would love to take a lot of computer classes. I feel that in society and in the future the world will be ran by computers. Becoming a future business man, I will need to know all I can know.

While I'm in college I would also like to participate sports such as; basketball. I think playing sports will help me to become a better team player. The other benefit to playing sports is that I would have less free time to get into negative situations.

Once I finish college I plan to use my business skills by running a business and providing jobs for people in the community. I also plan to coach the youth. I also plan to participate in civic organizations such as YMCA. I hope my contribution will make the world a better place to live in.

$1R Nuncio

73

A Future Consideration

As I stare across the field into the cowboy-blue skies

Wishing I had someone to confide in,

Knowing your world is where I long to lie

Not so much as a lover but more than a friend!

It's more to you than the naked eye can see

Experience tells me only time will tell,

Intuition and energy vibes lead me to believe

It'll be worth the wait to see

How great our destiny will be!

Enjoying our balanced scale of similarities

$1R Nuncio

While embracing our ambitions to succeed at the highest degree,

It just so happens we both value trust, honesty, and loyalty

I'm sure this is a future consideration for me!
12/11/2003

$1R Nuncio

74

A Friend Like Me

Just a phone call away at any time of the day

There is nothing I wouldn't do for you, there's no price I wouldn't pay!

Appreciative of your company, I cherish every single second spent

It wasn't until you weren't available, I realized how much to my life you meant!

Always with whatever whenever, as long as we're together

Willing to shelter you from any storm, be your umbrella when it rains

Just never forget our initial commitment

$1R Nuncio

Stay loyal to one another no matter how bad the weather!

Pursue success, I'm wit it!

Go against the grain, forget it!

If I lose all mine in route to gain yours

Until it's all said and done your best interest I'm committed!

Written: Sometime or another

75

One Route 2 Peace

When pleasure seeking, the young mind will grasp ahold the first, easiest pastime it gets influenced by; therefore, positive influences, good living environments, safe places to socialize, and the importance of education needs to be instilled properly on a regular basis at a young age preferably between the ages of 9-14. Before a society can be united as one, peace within individuality has to come about first. A solid foundation based on abiding by God's law and treating others how you want to be treated needs to be professed thoroughly at home.

Good intentions can, and will go wrong if not executed! So not only do we have to conjure up positive goals to achieve within reasonable reality, we have to stay dedicated until the job is completely finished. Keep in mind that your faith will be tested because everything worth having is worth fighting and striving for. Know that if you stay in control of your emotional state of being and consciously aware of your ultimate goal(s), you are sure to prevail.

1/16/2004

$1R Nuncio

76

Who Would Of Known

Anticipating a peace of mind while reminiscing on the past,

Always in route of success despite experiencing plenty of setbacks,

Never knowing exactly when, but sure to receive my desired blessings,

Being that man has counterfeited fraud to its highest degree,

Quicker to observe in totality before plunging forward,

Staying conscientiously aware of what's best for me!

Aspiring to possess the complete package knowing statistically it's likely to happen,

When profits outweigh the risk and duties override the beauty, get it craccin'!

Fearless of the unknown and prepared for the occasion,

Who would of known that my dream would come true in the stickiest situation!

When you can't be the highway, be a trail!

When you can be a sun be a star!

MLK Day 2004

$1R Nuncio

77

Almost There

Though your vision expresses many blessings,

Still a lot of doubt due to no answers to particular questions;

So pleasing & promising when promoting your pledge,

Still evaluating the facts to see if it's best that I did...

Maybe it's my own fears and insecurities

That won't allow me to be what you want me to be,

~Leaving no stone unturned in my pursuit to attain the bed of roses,

Not quite sure if your blueprint notarizes success ~

However, your poetic insight does keep me focused!

$1R Nuncio

Up the creek without a paddle

~yet your devotion instills harmony in my heart

Within sight of conviction still questioning when to start

Witnessing plenty counterfeit commitments

It's so hard to believe you got me by a narrow squeak!

X-Mas Eve 2003

78

Special

Not too many spirits stay uplifted like yours

Even after all you been through and all that attempted to keep you down,

You still continue to soar!

I honor your continuous ambition to keep smiling through life's trials

Incredible how you manage to be joyful on this marathon

When the average couldn't cope a single lap, let alone many miles!

Keep doing what you doing, your testimony is one needed to be heard,

I know it ain't nothin' like some reassurance

$1R Nuncio

That's why I transformed the love in my heart into these beautiful words;

You are really someone special

2/3/2004

$1R Nuncio

79

Your Smile

From the moment I witnessed your smile,

I was shell-shocked from the warmth overwhelming my body at that point

For you, I know I'd walk that extra mile!

Knowing it's more behind your beauty

I anticipate to know the unknown truth

Despite the rumor "the package is never complete"

Most definitely you got me with the nerve of your truth!

Both engaged to a world that some don't approve,

Being totally opposites I'm wondering how will we connect;

There's no doubt we'll make it happen

$1R Nuncio

Cuz the greatest qualities we both possess!

What kind of man would I be if I kept these thoughts of interest to myself?

The proof is in the pudding!

I'm pretty sure you know the recipe; here I am, all the ingredients you'll need

Whenever you're ready, I'll be waiting on the shelf!

Study long study wrong, I advise it wouldn't be wise to wait awhile

Know that I'm willing to dedicate 50% of every day just to make you smile!

"It's sumthin' bout your smile"

4/21/2004

$1R Nuncio

80

The One

Just fine as May wine, your one of a kind self

Most strive to have an experience with you recorded up under their belt!

Extraordinary attention-getter, so seductive with your vision;

Great eye-candy to the public, gotta be one of the best that God's given!

"Whomever said, "all that glitters ain't gold"

Couldn't have been speaking of you,

Cuz behind closed doors you're prettier than a Bahamas ocean view!

Blessed with the genes anyone in their right mind would love to clone,

And since God so loved the world you gotta be the one in my home!

4/24/2004

81

Why Not You?

Always smiling and smelling delicious

"Ms. I don't even need any makeup!"

Knowing you do so little to look so good,

I see why they stare like that!

By any means necessary,

Always willing to do everything in your power!

Don't ever get loud talking reckless

And keep a nigga laughing!

Had an opportunity to leave me drowning yet you called for rescue,

And jumped in to save me yourself!

Receptive to my plans from the gate

And never once did you not follow my lead!

Look at all you've sacrificed for the welfare of us...

Ms.-I stayed around throughout the bad times,

What I look like leaving you now!

4/24/04

$1R Nuncio

82

I Do, I Don't, I Won't, I Will!

So what, everybody don't think you're cute, "I Do!"

So what, if everything you do for us they don't approve, "I Do!"

So what, they don't believe we share true love, "I Do!"

So what, if they can't picture us rising above, "I Do!"

I don't.. believe in outsiders having a say in our dealings!

I don't.. like you considering others' influencing your feelings!

I don't.. entertain any moves not benefiting us!

I don't.. ever want you to stop giving me your love!

I won't.. ever break the trust & bond we secured!

I won't.. forget the ongoing stamina of dedication endured!

I won't.. follow any directions not in route to our goals!

I won't.. allow physical separations to hinder me from loving you more!

Who will always stick with the commitment made? "I Will!"

Who gone quench your thirst for Anything if you dehydrate? "I Will!"

Who might do *whateva* you like just to see you smile? "I Will!"

4/25/2004

$1R Nuncio

83

Beauty

Beauty..

Is something most would love to possess

Is pure

Isn't conjured up with fictitious ingredients and covered with artificial dressings

Beauty..

Attracts unwanted attention at times

Causes jealousy & envy

Is a quality which ignites sexual desire

Beauty..

Is not an illusion

Makes you wanna _____?

Inspires many to think creatively

$1R Nuncio

Beauty..

Is sometimes more than what the naked eye can see

Can be what you make it

Might bring the best out of you

Beauty..

Can be easily destroyed

Could be quite dangerous

Is enjoyed by most, but for some odd reason is hated by many!

"You're so Beautiful!"

4/29/2004

84

From Me 2 You

True love doesn't disappear when unfortunate situations occur.

I hope you won't allow our temporary physical separations to forfeit your benefits.

I see it's true when they say looking for loyalty is like signing on a blank check!?

We'll never prosper as long as you're holding me accountable for your last significant other's faults!

Timing is always of the essence so it's best that you capitalize on this opportunity while you still can!

I thought you knew better and would do better, but it seems as if you're no different from the rest!

But all of a sudden.. (shall be continued)

5/21/2004

$1R Nuncio

85

My Everythang

The cold-blooded naked truth,

The love something like a mothers,

The spiral I could never throw,

The sex I always lusted,

The child I have yet to father,

The game-winning touchdown I didn't score,

The platinum selling album I've yet record,

The last day of school before summer vacation,

The hot shower after a couple of games of ball,

The winning lottery ticket I should've bought,

The convicting evidence to my unsolved mystery,

The word on the tip of my tongue always coming to mind,

The decision to grant my freedom after years of incarceration,

My Everythang!   5/27/04

86

None Other Than

Been glowing ever since our initial greeting;

A player I would never want to trade to another; team

Associates even question the difference in my smile;

Something like that glimpse of ecstasy in your wildest dream!

Contract renewal guaranteed long before its expiration date;

Haven't been a day yet you haven't given 132%;

Might as well go blind, nothing else I need to see;

Who would of known so young so content I would be!

$1R Nuncio

Genuinely affectionate, you always cool my burning desires;

Mentally, Spiritually, Emotionally, & Physically discombobulated

When out of sight and not in your presence;

No doubt it's you I call on when it's down to the wire!

Alone together, with no outside influences;

A feeling better than freedom to a life sentenced convict!

Can't trust anyone with this one, wanna keep it to myself;

Best believe it's you I adore and will always cherish!

5/27/2004

$1R Nuncio

87

Pleasure Seeking

Tense, due to it being the first approach

Still wanting to proceed with intentions to conquer

Slightly timid cuz' of the possibility of failure

Hoping the signs observed of success aren't deceiving my vision!

Grand appearance, such a beautiful sight

Seems as if heaven went on recess

and allowed the angels to come out and play!

The motivation to be entwined with your soul is for real!

Sub-conscience interviews now filled with doubts of loss

$1R Nuncio

If a goal isn't accomplished, subject to suffer

If the plan is executed, much wealth and peace

Only thing left to do now is pursue!

Hoping the Queen will favor the request of her presence

What a good look and bright future ahead!

Eggs are scrambled, butter has gotten hard, jello has jiggled;

With the shot clock counting down the only option left is to

Shoot my best shot and hope for the best!

5/27/2004

$1R Nuncio

88

What's Next

You know what you did right?

Worked me up an appetite only you can fulfill

Will I be life starving?

I'll find a way to distract my hunger for you until you come through!

Should I hold my breath?

I know you aren't gonna let me suffocate to death!

How long will you leave me anxiously waiting with impatience?

Being the man I am I can cope, but for how long I don't know.

$1R Nuncio

Did you know you could cause such a feeling?

I'm glad but curious how it dawned upon me

Do you also question if it was meant to be or just another coincidence?

Everything happens for a reason so I believe!

All of a sudden we meet in this form of fashion!

I've heard of dreams coming true and prayers being answered,

Will we forfeit the benefits, or capitalize on this opportunity?

On my last breath of wind, I hope you bring me oxygen!

5/29/2004

89

Blind to the Fact

I would hate to go on with memories of should've would've could've

So every approach in a respectful manner will be taken from now on;

With no rejection from the gate, success is up for grabs

Now more clever deliveries are in the making!

Various signs of achievement, or my perfect illusion?

Is kindness being taken for weakness I question my conclusion.

Scoreboard unavailable for reading, unaware if I'm losing

Can't wait for a direct response to cancel the confusion!

$1R Nuncio

Haven't heard a fat lady sing so I guess there's still a chance,

More than likely the requested parties are balancing their options;

Is that my song playing with an opportunity to dance all life?

Probably the best bet is to move with caution!

Never going crazy not knowing if I'm accepted or rejected,

Will I get what I wished for if I just kick back?

Adrenaline rushing, & blood pumping; where is this headed?

It's a cold feeling being blind to the fact!

"Why me?"

6/4/2004

90

My Badd

Never knew love could cause so much pain

While parlaying, neither could picture being the recipient of its failure

Certain emotions are better left unexpressed in order to make spiritual progress

The vital information held sacred was just a form of being careful!

How far could we have gone with all the cards played from the start

No intentions to deceive, don't ever want to part

Only want to fulfill the empty space in your heart

By any means necessary I have to be number #1 on your chart!

Fearing rejection, I admit to withholding convicting evidence

Confused on which approach to proceed with, the lie descends deeper

My chance of glory, I sense you're heaven sent

I just have to please you!

A code was broken that we just can't ignore,

Do we move on and cancel our previous plans?

Consider our precious, valuable, unforgettable times a waste?

With another chance we promise to do all we can!

God is forgiving and summer school is available to redeem the past semester

I succeeded my probation period, aren't I subject to suspension before termination?

Always keep in mind everything happens for a reason..

Before finalizing your conclusion, all I ask is to

$1R Nuncio

Remember my love, sacrifice, and dedication!

6/5/2004

$1R Nuncio

91

Mother Dearest

Through life threatening storms,

To nursing the wounds when cowards swarmed,

My #1 supporting cast throughout numerous trips of incarceration,

While watching me rush, you always kept your patience!

When hurting from crying, you still keep faith in prayers

Sacrificing daily for the sake of your seeds,

In desperate need of a vacation, you always work even harder

Does literally "whatever" to ensure your children are at peace!

When instructions aren't obeyed, disciplinary actions take place

Chores completed on initiative bring an ear to ear smile on your face

Company always enjoyable, so much warmth in your hugs

I'm talking cutting pancakes and peeling oranges, a true mothers love!

Too concerned at times, but of course worrying is one duty of a mother

Tries to never show favoritism between the sisters & brothers;

Despite the rank of your career; shelter, food and clothing was always provided

Whether followed or not, a route to success was guided!

None other than the most appreciated woman in MY world,

For all you've done & wanted to do

$1R Nuncio

I thank you Mother, and love you even more!

I love you so!

6/7/2004

$1R Nuncio

92

Facts of Our Life

Poverty-struck duckin' the law, vast flagrant tragedies are witnessed. Lost as an adolescent prior to sophistication, bogus expeditions were entertained. Led astray with no patience by idol minds, peep the life that is sought camouflaging the Devil's attributes. It's not too surprising that by 13 yrs of age engaging with the crime society is in full effect, and by 15 turning 4 plus calendars in the youth authority etching the first bid in stone. Entwining with the divine it takes a revocation of freedom to see the light. Remaining loyal to principles and talents in the midst of all this isn't an easy call, however keeping a balanced code of communication while running the streets has to hold firm.

In sticky situations, who's trustworthy when death is near and there's no fear? Is it God's love or Heckler the main-protector saving lives when enemies rush? Motivated by the root of all evil, it's us who strive for what currency can do for our lust. Dedicated to ambitions which outcomes are big

$1R Nuncio

bucks, yet sometimes we unconsciously destruct because we're often deprived of our freedom prior to having the opportunity to fully focus on the responsibilities that come with a wealthier lifestyle. Instead of succumbing to the bullshit that the ghetto life guides for our kind, we must believe it's possible to persevere through these times. i.e. look deeply at your past and current life. If it's meant to be, be patient for it'll surely happen.

$1R Nuncio

93

Only You

Blossoming from one of the sexiest cultures,

How could anyone not acknowledge the blessing
from above;

Disregarding all rumors & stereotypes,

Your presence deserves nothing but love!

While some describe your mysteriousness as weird,

I define your unique demeanor as sexy, smooth,
smart, and quite appealing;

Very appreciative to have met you

Whether it was meant to be, or pure happenstance!

Being one who realizes everyone isn't for everyone,

My thoughts of you won't be altered if rejected, and

$1R Nuncio

A full-throttle embrace isn't expected,

Just hoping my advance into your personal space isn't neglected!

So far so good

And better it can only get,

Only wanting this sincere approach to be seriously considered!!

8/6/04

94

Acme

Recall the feeling one second prior to your first climax!

Imagine the rush after cashing a million-dollar check!

Ponder completing the transaction for the purchase of the car of your dreams!

A situation occurrs that notarizes your significant other is down for anything!

The state when you realize you don't have a care in the world!

The time when your girl makes all ten toes curl!

When you accomplished the goal they said you couldn't!

$1R Nuncio

When you actually did what they said you wouldn't!

Seeing for yourself what you thought didn't exist!

The remedy conjured up so you would no longer get pissed!

When you find out the tragic incident is a lie and so far from the truth!

When you stop procrastinating and finally do everything you're supposed to!

~The Utmost Point of entertainment= Acme~

9/3/2005

95

The Prize in My Eyes

The sparkle in your eyes always ignites the fire inside of me!

Just a temporary breeze from your beauty blows away a bundle of pain,

The slightest touch of your tender caress

Makes a statement I forever want to say!

Since different origins prolonged our initial greeting,

Let's not disregard this moment to make magic;

Be sedate about decisions concerning me,

Be the recipient of a great relation between two fine breeds!

$1R Nuncio

The nation's ratings give us two thumbs up,

My side of the story suggests you see for yourself

Just to guarantee you feel all of the glory!

Will I be denied or shrugged off due to a few past bad habits,

Or will my access be granted to view your hidden talents?

It ain't really a long shot, just probably something slightly different

I just hope you take heed to the picture be presented!

If I'm not blessed to receive the gift of you, you'll never be forgotten

Cuz my eyes stay on the prize until it's all dead and rotten!

PS: "still looks alive and fresh to me!"

1/23/06

$1R Nuncio

96

Gangsta Reality

Adolescent years ain't nothing nice with so much hatred temptation,

And every time the mind is spoken it is criticized about decisions in the making!

Repressed emotions keep attitudes jacked up!

Hoping it'll make life a 'lil easier, sorrows get drowned in alcoholic bottles

Furthermore, commence to blazing the weed up!

Persistent to bang, unaware of destiny

Expected to die by the age of 25 is what they keep saying!

It's hard to maintain composure when they consider you a failure,

$1R Nuncio

Mistakes made from immaturity is how they compare you!

Dedicated to your ambitions rebelling against the system,

Demanding respect instantly cuz Gangsta Reality is all you see!

Not knowing all you know how to do is take penitentiary chances,

They'll never be able to understand the realism of ghetto circumstances!

$1R Nuncio

97

You Tell Me!

Led astray prior to knowing the severity of criminal consequences,

"Am I destined to be committed to life in the streets!?"

So eager to be stimulated by controlled substances,

"Did immaturity really play a part in my decision making!?"

Confined after an unsuccessful attempt to indulge in various ghetto lifestyles,

"I never had a choice but to experience what I did!" or did I?

$1R Nuncio

Being loved, liked, hated, respected, accepted, and rejected,

Accounts for my present need to have neither!

Born & raised in the church, influenced to believe in a certain religion which

Justifies my open mindset to possibly believe otherwise!

How could a firsthand victim of disloyalty,

Trust in another outside of the family?

"You Tell Me!"

2/20/2006

98

To Each's Own

More than I initially planned to have you, you're constantly on my mind every day!

Always needing you within reach, although you do cause a lot of attention at times!

Forever keeping a smile on my face,

Knowing you're in my life I sleep at peace with not many worries!

Fasure to be the talk of the town once the word gets around that you on my team,

And don't mind sharing you at all
as long as the night falls with you home with me!

Felt so right the first time I held you,

$1R Nuncio

I know I have to act accordingly if I plan to have you in my future!

Highly preferred,

Any male in his right mind can't live without you!

Though you cause a lot of unnecessary problems,

Probably the #1 reason for relationship breakups,

You still seem to always please!

"I'm talkin' bout legal tender!"

2/23/06

99

1 Of 'Dem Ones

Being known for your delicious demeanor,

Who in their right mind doesn't wanna dwell in your presence forever and ever!

Like the sun itself, everyone needs some of you in their life;

That is if they prefer to stay balanced and on top of their A-game!

For the umpteenth time,

you're my heart's favorite desire, emotions' best comforter, and hormones most wanted!

$1R Nuncio

Average,
is at the bottom of the totem pole when in company
with your good looks and swagger!

A divine creation, blessing every presence
encountered

Leaving no doubt in anyone's mind, simply
#unfucwitable!

2/23/06

$1R Nuncio

100

Right Up My Alley

Damn! Flawless to the T!

For the first time, I agree it's exactly what it seems to be!

Spectacular, fabulous, all that it could possibly be!

Authentic, genuine, and pure as Christmas is supposed to be merry!

Exquisitely gorgeous, so dazzling.. just marvelous!

Gradually reaching Godliness, honestly heavenly!

Surprisingly, you're compatible with my driven imagination,

And as much time as I've spent alone pondering

$1R Nuncio

I had to give our similarities an outstanding ovation!

Overwhelmed that the melody of your swagger is in tune with mine

I wanna make you forever mine, 'cuz you're always on my mind!

1/28/06

$1R Nuncio

101

When Will It Cease

(The violence, the guns, the fraud, the drugs, the drama, the gangbangin', the betrayal, the racism, etc.)

At the rate we are going, probably never! It is sad to say but statistically these times have made me a true believer. Although we are born to die, it is messed up that we have to suffer so much during our temporary stay on earth. Being that this is a cold world, it is so hard to chill. Sometimes I dread the future of our next generation. Knowing the wickedness and unfortunate situations our children will encounter in the near future, I always question whether I want to have children or not. Life is so beautiful at times that I feel motivated to breed my genes, but then again I reconsider the trials and tribulations to come. I have just as much hope as serious doubt for every child's sake.

Even with all the above existing today, I do believe there is reason to stay positively motivated

$1R Nuncio

to do the right thing and live life abundantly while having to be here. Overcoming being desensitized to negativity and not having a righteous care in the world, I actually live now to see us congregate in love, peace, and harmony. Why? because I'm aware of the benefits that come with true love, loyalty, positive reassurance, and trust due to experiencing the fates of living with a tunnel vision full of pessimism.

Often at times we fail to realize that when we commit violent acts and/or break moral codes we not only harm ourselves and any involved party, but we damage the security of our community. It is crazy how most beefs do not cease until a trigger release, and even then it only continues to cook the beef. The majority of hearts broken (due to violations of personal bonds) do not make amends and just never learn to trust or love again. Understanding that the game is to be played from that angle, we often wonder whether or not to continue playing by the original rules. With a lot of resentment towards the opposed, alongside the lack of communication between the two, we often lose faith in achieving the ultimate goal legitimately.

102

132 Days until

Almost there, and so many troubles attempt to intervene with future plans. By any means necessary get the money, right? Whatever it takes to get the cake, huh? Do all that is needed in order to stay on track with the original blueprint because anything else would be uncivilized. Since previous decisions account for one's current predicament, certain actions cannot be repeated when looking to revel in success. After assessing every option alongside balancing the profits and risks, which hustle is really worth it?

Knowing timing is always of the essence, recalculate how much time is wasted when entertaining the wrong things. Do not prolong your journey any longer with acts of foolishness. Be a wise, intelligent individual continuing to do what is required to reach your designated destiny. Those who truly love you and everything you stand for will support you no matter what the opposition thinks because they know you have a purpose behind every decision made and activity participated in. The

$1R Nuncio

ultimate goal is to only make moves that will result in a significant difference towards upgrading your financial wellbeing. With all of this in mind there should not be any more debates about your next move.

PS: may blessings rain upon you for making the correct choice!

103

Yours Truly

Honestly, tell me what you think of me.

Do you honestly tell yourself that WE could be?

More than you ever imagined, unlimited amounts of pleasure

Alongside an ongoing stamina of love & loyalty!

Literally, can you believe?

We can be happy as one until we no longer breathe!

Able to do all of which we ever wanted without constraints, and bound only by our eager to please!

Basically, if you do unto me as I do you

We'll always be together, just as the sky is forever one shade of blue!

$1R Nuncio

Really, with all B.S. to the side..

What legitimate reason is there to search deeper?

Look any further? Give someone else a chance?

To be in heaven on earth appreciating your woman's worth (cuz that's what it is being with you!)

To top it off, you know damn well this type of shit happens once in a lifetime

(I'm referring to the beneficial bond we've established!)

Let's embrace this with all our will, cherish it with all our heart!

Please stop me when I begin lying!

$1R Nuncio

104

If

If you're curious about my steelo, then get to know me when I provide the opportunity

If you consider taking that extra step and I'm asking you to go for the gusto hoping for the best,

"Don't keep hesitating to take that leap of faith!"

If you like me, stop acting like you don't &

If you got luv me, stop acting like you just like me a 'lil bit &

If you truly adore me, quit actin' like you just got a 'lil luv for me &

If I mean the world to you, quit actin' like it's just plain 'ol puppy love.

"Quit 42 fakin'! and hike and go long!"

232

$1R Nuncio

If everything happens for a reason, why stay in denial like fate didn't bring us together.

_If_ you know better then do better, so I won't think you're the ultimate bullshitter!

105

Daily Insight

Knowing everyone wants to feel important, we must remember not to be degrading with our mouths nor allow feelings to express anything hastily before our superior. Do not procrastinate about paying a debt, rather do not make promises and/or vow to do anything that cannot be guaranteed by your own power. The opposition has no pleasure in false commitment! It is better not to commit than to commit and not follow through.

About money and power.. *money does not care who owns it*! A bum can win it in the lottery, it can be inherited, or someone can hold up a bank to get it! But *power is different*! To have power is to own your world, not just exist amongst the population. He who fights the monster must remember not to become a monster while fighting the monster. When dealing with delicate situations, it is best to handle it from an "outside the box" perspective. Do not jump inside the box with the problem! Very few will be loyal, so be cautious with whom is chosen as a confidante. That smile is probably dying to see a frown on you, so do your homework before you get

$1R Nuncio

involved with anyone, *even* if they are from your side of town.

$1R Nuncio

106

Fraud

The truth only hurts the fake!

"We Americans have camouflaged fraud to its highest degree to the point in which we cannot even tell the difference between real or fake anymore"

Ex. I attended a racism workshop class and each student defined racism differently. Too many grey areas and different perspectives about significant ground rules and codes of conduct these days

"Take heed to the fact that everything is not always what it seems to be, and everyone isn't who they claim to be"

I truly believe that before we devote any significant amount of time, notarize our decisions, make a commitment, or engage in any act which the results are life threatening we should do our personal research to ensure ourselves that everything is

$1R Nuncio

kosher. Based on we are emotional creatures we tend to act upon instinct more than logic, and that is not always the best manner to deal with the vast majority of encounters we face daily. So many individuals in these times camouflage with the (in-crowd) and blanket their true colors. I have difficulty believing anything I hear, a third of what I read, and half of what I see! *Do not get it twisted* and think information all comes in one ear and goes in one ear and out the other. It is just that I think rationally and act logically far more than I do emotionally.

Paying close attention to the core of things existing today and influencing our future, it is clear to see how love, money, and morals have been duplicated in an ugly fashion that is truly unbelievable. Our attraction to materialistic possessions is ridiculous, and it distracts us from the authenticity of an individual. Take notice to the double standard abused in most relationships. (It is cool for us and not for them) attitude encompasses our thought process. There is no doubt in my mind that we cannot view, judge, or deal with acts the same when it comes to man or woman, but some things are being taken advantage of because of one's sex and that is not a good enough reason to justify the wrongdoing committed.

Nowadays, love for one another depends on how much money is spent and how soon something is done for the other. We as a people have forgotten or are unaware of the true definition and everything it represents. When priorities change, our perspectives, morals, and values change right along with them. Although most of us mean well, we tend to lose some focus during strenuous situations and not respond accordingly because of various other factors in our lives. From drug usage to unhealthy co-parenting, we must not permit our hardships to negatively influence our behaviors. As I always love to say, *"we must stay consciously aware at all times in every kind of situation"*.

<u>107</u>

<u>Temptations/Influences</u>

Whether one would enjoy admitting it or not, we all are influenced by our surroundings in one way or another. We all are tempted to exploit the nearest accepted pastime(s). It is very important that we ensure our children are raised in positive environments. Unfortunately, there will always be negativity existing, but the least we can do to keep it to a minimum is surround ourselves with in a positive community living productive lifestyles. If the activities witnessed on a daily basis are accepted and glamorized by one's peers, it will be extremely difficult not to give some a try at least once. Too much free time on a child's hands will leave no choice but to consider exploring the world around. Pleasure seeking as an immature teenager can be dangerous for a child's future because if the experimented activity is enjoyed before or without punishment, it will become habitual due to the instant gratification received. *We all know how bad habits are hard to break!*

$1R Nuncio

Even with the right guide to success provided within the home by parents, the young mindset seems to be more drawn towards believing everything can be executed in his/her own way. Parents have to keep in mind to thoroughly explain intricate details in terms of the present. The right teachings have to be comprehended properly because the understanding of past generations is not always parallel with the advancement in today's world. Picture being groomed in the greater Los Angeles area during the height of the gangbang & crack cocaine epidemic by parents 37 years your senior who were raised in the south & back east in the midst of the civil rights movement...? (*Think about it now*)

In any period of time, actions speak louder than words! If you are preaching (complete school and find gainful, *not a career*) while living below average and right at or above the poverty line still struggling to pay rent, driving an old car nor can you afford to miss a day's work; it is likely the child experiencing this form of upbringing will seek another lifestyle to live and most likely it will be one which generates money the fastest. Once children mature, eventually they will understand where you were coming from even if they find themselves heavily involved in a wicked lifestyle and experience some traumatizing events. It is best that we provide righteous examples for our next generation to follow

$1R Nuncio

instead of constantly allowing society to dictate our children's future - that is if we really want to see our next generation of people reach new heights of success. Social media, television, radio programs, magazines, etc. messages are not always conceived properly and exercised the way we would wish them to be; furthermore, it is best to stay on top of everything catching our youth's attention and be there to help them fight the negative influences in a manner that will not be rebelled against. Just make sure the true meaning of what is being expressed is understood.

108

Free to a Certain Extent

*(Especially for those in physical bondage & in the prison of their minds, **I feel your pain!**)*

What does this mean and have to do with me is what most probably are wondering while reading the title of this passage. I cannot blame you! This passage is more so for individuals who have been incarcerated and are trying to succeed on parole, or people who are seeing life with tunnel vision not having the slightest idea where they are headed. For the sake of your curiosity, as I write I am part of this coexistence.

Being that I am not a regular citizen due to currently being on California Youth Authority parole, I am constantly reminded of my status in every situation I face. I am not allowed to congregate with my friends, and although I am of age to legally drink alcohol I cannot without the consequence of a negative urinalysis. I can no longer visit my community recreational park, and when

$1R Nuncio

encountering law enforcement I am subject to a suspect's search. Certain violations which may get the average American citizen a ticket, I can be incarcerated. And the list goes on.. not that it is impossible, but I admit that it is extremely difficult to succeed legitimately when forced to abide by three sets of laws while not being established in life due to being incarcerated one-third of your life.

Picture being deprived of your freedom as an adolescent and placed back into the gangbang capital of the world at the tender age of twenty without a dime, car, clothes, significant other, legal resources, prison education/job experience only, strict parole conditions, and a time constraint on when to succeed. Crazy, right!? Hmmm! Note that family is in a financial crisis as well so food is not even free.

*Well.. if you are reading this, I have prevailed. More hardships were experienced before I got to this point of my life. I truly hope this was a great read for you and your love ones. **Thanks for taking the time to grasp my vibe.***

109

Life..

Be proud of your cleanliness,

Love thy self!

Don't be selfish nor too reckless,

Enjoy your wealth!

Stay persistent when pursuing goals,

Keep the faith!

Regardless how you do it,

Someone will always hate!

If patience is a virtue, virtue must be a rare breed,

Cuz so many are impatient, virtue must be near extinct!

Whether hardly working or working hard,

Satisfactory completion in a timely manner is only important!

$1R Nuncio

Money isn't everything supposedly,

But we're labeled as failures if we can't afford it!

Too much of anything isn't good for you,

But still most are greedy!

There's more will to help those who have,

And less motivation to assist the needy!

Fraud has been camouflaged to its highest degree

Be extra cautious when notarizing what's real or fake!

Born with the blessing to decide for ourselves of course

Rules, commitments, and promises were meant to break!

Acknowledgements

First & foremost, I want to thank God for giving me life and making all things possible. I love you mother (Mary Dykes) & father (Walter Dykes) for being the vessel responsible for my life on earth. Shelly, my Big Sis, I love you girl! Thanks for Always having my back during every circumstance! Rest In Peace Magoo! (My Brother Shae McGee). You're entwined in everything I do. I miss you and love you bro! My brother Ashanti, sister Tracy, nieces Yasmine & Tish, nephews Shae'on, and Rylen, I love you all dearly along with the rest of my family members I know personally and those I have never met. Unfortunately yet a blessing in disguise, all the enclosed literature was written during various stints of incarceration. I want my readers to know that being physically confined didn't stop me mentally. *Facilities which housed me and provoked this literature: California Youth Authority: Fred C. Nelles, Heman G. Stark Youth Training School, Ventura, Preston, DeWitt Nelson, and Mt. Bullion. Washington State Correctional Centers: Washington State Penitentiary (Walla Walla), Clallum Bay, McNeil Island, and Airway Heights. I wanna give a special shout out to my day1 Leron Carter bka Baby Birdlegs aka Pimpin Birdd for the inspiration & encouragement to live differently under city lights, and for being the sole creator of our "GARR" slogan. My L & R's to my intellectual partner Benjale Cushon bka Baby Underdogg R90NHC aka I-KO$$ Tha Money Boss who was present during the creation of and my transformation into $1R Nuncio. Also, I wanna give another special thanks to my big homie Lil Birdlegs aka MP for being #Nutty and always lacing me wit sum real game while keeping me

$1R Nuncio

dying-laughing. And my Folks Poochie from Seattle, WA who encouraged me to finish my novel "In This Dirrty Game" when I was halfway done and didn't wanna continue. It's coming next! I want to thank all the rest of my friends (female & male) not mentioned by name (DON'T BE MAD IF YOUR NAME ISN'T MENTIONED SPECIFICALLY), my extended family: the West Side Gardena 132nd x 139th street Shotgun Crips, business associates, and playa partners all across the states for the support, encouragement, and love thus far. You know who you are, let's keep it lit! Best wishes to my readers!

$1R Nuncio